WAR, PROGRESS, AND THE END OF HISTORY

INCLUDING A SHORT STORY
OF THE ANTI-CHRIST

THREE
DISCUSSIONS
BY
VLADIMIR SOLOVIEV

Translated from the Russian by
ALEXANDER BAKSHY

With a Biographical Notice by
DR. HAGBERG WRIGHT

London : University Of London Press

PUBLISHED FOR THE UNIVERSITY
OF LONDON PRESS, LTD.
BY HODDER & STOUGHTON, WARWICK
SQUARE, LONDON, E.C.

1915

CONTENTS

Biographical Notice...1

Translator's Preface..5

Author's Preface...9

Three Discussions...23

The First Discussion. 25

The Second Discussion. 59

The Third Discussion. 105

A Short Story Of The Anti-Christ. 145

BIOGRAPHICAL NOTICE.

B Y the early death of Vladimir Soloviev in 1900 Russia lost her most original and essentially Slavonic thinker. A deep sympathy with mysticism, united to the power of fearlessly probing human consciousness,] gave him eminence not only among the philosophers of Russia, but of Europe.

Born in 1853, Soloviev entered upon life in an atmosphere charged with the elements of change. The emancipation of the serfs opened an era of political experiments, and the ordeal of the Crimean War braced and stimulated the national spirit. It was a time of high aspirations struggling against an undercurrent of philosophic doubt, which exercised an abiding influence upon the sensitive and inquir- ing mind of Soloviev.

He was happy in his parentage; his father, Serge Soloviev, being a historian of high reputation, and his mother a woman of character and mental attain- ments. She belonged to a noble family of Little Russia, and numbered among her ancestors a great- uncle who had won consideration as a philosophic writer; from this source possibly Soloviev derived the bent of his intellect.

The period of his education in a school at Moscow was marked by a series of brilliant successes, and at its conclusion he was presented with the rare distinction of a gold medal. His university career was no less remarkable.

The faculty of Natural Sciences soon proving less congenial than the study of history and phil- osophy, he devoted himself to the latter, and passed his candidate's examination (practically equivalent to our B.A.) in 1873.

The tendency of Soloviev's mind now became apparent. At the age of twenty he abandoned his secular studies and entered upon a twelve months' course in the theological college of Moscow. After a year chiefly devoted to the consideration of re- ligious questions, he went up to the University of St. Petersburg and took out his degree of M.A., f or which he wrote the thesis : The Crisis in Western Philosophy." Very shortly afterwards he was appointed assistant professor (P rival- do cent) in the University of Moscow, a position which he did not hold for long, being of a character to which freedom of action was essential.

Two subsequent years were spent in foreign travel when he visited England. Upon his return he was appointed a member of the committee of popular education.

His activity as a lecturer dates from that appoint- ment, and for the next four or five years Soloviev was engaged in lecturing on various philosophical and literary topics, such as "the Science of Re- ligion" and "the Literary Movement of the Nine- teenth Century." His most notable work, "The Criticism of Abstract Ideas," and his memorable address in condemnation of capital punishment both belong to this period.

In 1882, however, Soloviev relinquished the burden of a public career and gave up lecturing in order to devote himself wholly to literature and science. His restless and moody disposition, aggravated by habits of personal negligence and asceticism, made fixity of all kinds irksome, and he became a wanderer, residing sometimes in Moscow, sometimes in St. Petersburg, roaming from one country estate to another seeking by change of scene and companionship to keep despondency at bay.

Monasticism appealed strongly to Soloviev. The physical aspects of human existence aroused his contempt and aversion, and material comforts and pleasures were at all times matters of indifference to him. For months together he would lead the life of a recluse, cutting himself off entirely from the outside world. At such times he spent whole nights in writing and meditation, depriving himself of sleep and nourishment. Unhappily, his body was not slow to retaliate and assert its right to considera- tion. The greatest of Russian philosophers died on the thirty-first of July, 1900, at the premature age of forty-seven.

The full scope of Soloviev's philosophy cannot be traced within the limits of a prefatory note, but his life-work may be summed up in his own words as "a free inquiry into the foundations of human knowledge, life, and activity." At the same time, a close study of his writings reveals him as an idealist, a theologian, and a mystic. His ideal was the Christian one of love and self-denial, of uni- versal brotherhood as against Slavophilism. Of patriotism in the narrow sense he became the violent opponent, attacking the Slavophil writer, Danilev- sky, with impassioned eloquence, though, on the other hand, he felt unable to accept the doctrine of Tolstoy, which preaches the non-resistance of evil. To refute that doctrine, and emphasise the imminence of the struggle which he foresaw between East and West, Soloviev wrote the "Three Discussions," which were published in 1899 an d 190x3. This work is now for the first time brought to the attention of the English reading public. It forms an excellent example of the author's irony and humour, of his dialectic and power of self-expression.

Soloviev was the author of many volumes dealing with the Christian religion, the best known being "The Religious Foundations of Life" (1884). "The History and Future of Theocracy," and "The Dogmatic Development of the Church" (1886), in which he discusses the differences dividing the Greek and Roman Catholic Churches and the necessity for their union.

His philosophical works include a "History of Materialism" (1894), a "History of Ethics" (1896-8), and "The Justification of Good" (1897), which is one of his finest achievements.

Soloviev was also the author of poems, which breathe the true Slav spirit and are remarkable for their self-revelations. In them, more than in any other of his writings, we gain an insight into the character and feelings of a man whose life, in the words of Prince Trubetzkoy, was " full of yearning to justify his faith, to justify the good in which he believed ; the life of a wrestler ever seeking to over- come the dark forces of evil heaving in his breast." The cause of religion was dearer to him than the arid domain of pure logic. He avows his task to be "to justify the faith of our fathers, carrying it upward to a new plane of intellectual consciousness, and making manifest (the oneness of that ancient faith with eternal and universal truth, when it has been set free from the chains of dogma and temporal pride."

Soloviev was a true patriot. He loved his fellow- countrymen and he welcomed any personal sacrifice for the general good. He realised that education was the peasants' first and greatest need. Though a nationalist, he had a broad and tolerant mind, and championed the cause of religious freedom in a striking series of articles (1893 and 1894). His crowning merit lies in this, that, at a time when indifference to religion and spiritual thought pervaded the ranks of education and culture, he re- opened " the windows to eternal things."

The name of Soloviev may not be a household word in so wide a sense as the name of Tolstoy, but he holds a higher place as a thinker among the intellectual classes of Russia.

C. HAGBERG WRIGHT.

TRANSLATOR'S PREFACE

WE are living in a time when half the world is plunged in the bellicose element and the normal life of mankind has imbibed war as its natural com- ponent, which like a fluid has filled it to its farthest boundaries, penetrating everywhere, bringing its hydraulic pressure on every member of the human community, crushing and sweeping away the weak and unstable, and strengthening and consolidating those endowed with a more robust constitution— when, in a word, war has become a matter of every- day life and, in common with everyday occurrences, has restricted our attention to the events of to-day and the possible developments of to-morrow. At such a time a peculiar significance attaches to the voice of a philosopher who, by the power of his mighty spirit, is able to probe into the destinies of mankind farther than has been granted to others, and to whom a new and startling aspect of the purpose and meaning of human life has been revealed.

In a characteristically Russian manner, Vladimir Soloviev refuses to confine himself to the immediate bearings and aspects of the war- problem, but fear- lessly subjects it to examination *sub specieaeternitatis*. For him war is only a part of the more general question of fighting evil, and it is his original conception of evil which is the guiding principle in his analysis. It is impossible to go into the metaphysical theories of Soloviev here. A few explanations are, however, necessary, lest the reader, puzzled by the quaint and seemingly un- substantiated prophecies of future developments, should regard them as the product of an irre- sponsible mind given to fancies and hallucinations. "The Three Discussions" is not a creation of an inexperienced young man, whose youth could, per- haps, be held responsible for its " fantastic char- acter." On the contrary, it is the crowning achieve- ment, of the philosopher's life, embodying his last and final conclusions on the evolution and future of mankind.

Through all the works of Soloviev there runs one cardinal thought: the idea of the evolution of the world which has made humanity a factor in the life of Deity itself, has imbued it with God's spirit in the form of " God-human-ness" and has destined it for a final union with God "the all-unity" by overcoming that power which, though emanating from God, has severed itself from Him, has created the material world, and has been the cause of existing evil. The realisation of this process in the life of humanity, the ever-growing unity with God, was pictured by Soloviev differently at different periods of his life. There was a period when he believed that such a unity would be possible in this world, and that it would be accomplished by a transformation of the present-day states into a world theocracy. In this transformation a mission of special importance was assigned to Russia, who was believed to nourish within herself the idea of uni- versal salvation. Soloviev was not alone in these hopes of God's Kingdom on Earth, and of the mission of Russia in their realisation. He shared them and, moreover, practically worked them out in close co-operation with his friend, Dostoievsky, who, for his own part, gave expression to them in his famous novel, "The Brothers Karamazov." But towards the close of his life, Soloviev began to see things differently. No longer could he believe in the realisation of God's Kingdom in this world. Only by a complete victory over the world that is sunk in evil, only by a general resurrection of all living beings could the unity with the "All- One" be achieved. And this end will be attained, not through the union of the State and the Church, led and headed by the spiritual power of Russia, as he previously believed, but by means of the union of true Christians of all persuasions, righting against those who regard this world as the only Kingdom of God.

This idea forms the basis of his " Story of the Anti-Christ," and it will be observed that in his picture of the reign of the Anti-Christ he actually turns the weapons against himself and his former aspirations of God's Kingdom on Earth. But fear- less as this renunciation is, it is not presented altogether fairly in the "Three Discussions." Here Leo Tolstoy has been made the scapegoat of the philosopher's indignation. Apart from the truth of Soloviev's conception of evil and the Anti-Christ, which, of course, can be disputed on more grounds than one, the fact that Tolstoy, with his preaching non-resistance and moral perfection, is singled out as a forerunner of the Anti-Christ, shows all the signs of a bias, sincere and involuntary, no doubt, but nevertheless hardly justified in fact; particularly so in the light of Soloviev's own opinion that the element of Anti-Christ has been present in all the historical forms of Christianity, and, we may add, was not entirely absent from even his own system. This inconsistency, however, detracts very little from the value and significance of Soloviev's teaching. In whatever form a man's own intuition may assimilate the external world, whatever meta- physical conceptions may be built up on the basis of such intuition, one cannot help recognising that in Soloviev's philosophy an original and singularly profound aspect of the world finds an extremely lucid, consistent, and exhaustive presentation. The essential feature of Soloviev, as of all the Russian thinkers and, one would like to say, of all the spiritual life of Russia, is the earnestness, the burning spirit with which truth is sought and the aims of life are conceived and pursued. It is for this reason that a mere rational comprehension can never suffice for a full and true appreciation of a Russian thinker. To experience his truth one has to descend below the mechanism of his ideas to the abysses of his spirit where the eternal thirst for knowledge moulds itself into his individual perception of the world. Unfortunately, not every- body is capable of doing so, and just at present there is to be perceived a dangerous tendency to "superficialise," if one may say so, the hitherto much ignored spiritual life of Russia, in the attempt to present it to the eyes of the British public

TRANSLATOR'S PREFACE

: since the essential condition of appreciation is a personal experience, and the agony and vicissitudes of spiritual development seem to be little familiar to the greater number of would-be interpreters of the Russian soul. Yet it is this depth and earnestness that distinguish Russia as a nation. If any mission be at all assigned to her in the future destinies of Western Europe, it is not to deliver any particular message, but rather to stimulate and set aflame the slumbering spirit of the cultured world. "*Ex oriente lux*" the Slavophiles used to say—"*Ex oriente ignis* " would, perhaps, be more in conformity with the ardent spirit of Russia.

ALEXANDER BAKSHY.

Whilst translating the "Three Discussions," I have been fortunate enough to secure the assistance of a number of English friends, to whom I wish to record my great indebtedness. In particular, my thanks are due to Mr. Robert Finch, who has care- fully edited my manuscript; and to Mr. G. H. Green, who has helped me in the work of reading the proofs, and has also rendered Count Alexis Tol- stoy's verses into English metre, preserving, as far as possible, the grotesque character of the Russian original.

A. B.

AUTHOR'S PREFACE.

Is *evil* only a natural defect, an imperfection dis- appearing of itself with the growth of good, or is it a real *power*, possessing our world by means of temptations, so that for fighting it successfully assistance must be found in another sphere of being ? This vital question can be fully examined and solved only in a complete system of metaphysics.

I began carrying out this task for those who are capable of contemplation,[1] but I soon felt how im- portant the problem of evil is for everybody Some two years ago a change in the tenor of my spiritual life, which there is no need to dwell upon just now, created in me a strong and firm desire to illumine in some clear and easy way the main aspects of the problem of evil, which must concern everybody. For a long time I was unable to find a suitable medium for carrying out my plan. In the spring of 1899, however, during my stay abroad, I spontaneously composed and wrote in a few days the first discussion on this subject, and on returning to Russia wrote the two others. In this way I dis- covered the literary form which this work assumes,[1] The introduction to this work was published by me in the first three chapters of my "Theoretical Philosophy." and which provided me with the simplest medium for the expression of the thoughts I was desirous of communicating. This form of drawing-room dis- cussion is a sufficient proof in itself that neither a scientifico-philosophical examination nor

AUTHOR'S PREFACE.

an ortho- dox sermon should be looked for in this work. My object in it was rather apologetic and polemic : I endeavoured, as far as I could, to set out clearly and prominently the vital aspects of Christian truth, in so far as it is connected with the question of evil, and to disperse the fog with which everybody seems to have been trying lately to enwrap it.

Many years ago I happened to read about a new religion that was founded in the eastern provinces of Russia. The religion, the followers of which called themselves "Hole-drillers," or "Hole- worshippers," was very simple; a middle-sized hole was drilled in a wall in some dark corner of a house, and the men put their mouths to it and repeated earnestly: "My house, my hole, do save me!" Never before, I believe, has the object of worship been reduced to such a degree of simplicity. It must be admitted, however, that though the worship of an ordinary peasant's house, and of a simple hole made by human hands in its wall, was a palpable error, it was a truthful error; those men were abso- lutely mad, but they did not deceive anybody; the house they worshipped they called a house, and the hole drilled in the wall they reasonably termed merely a *hole*.

But the religion of the hole-worshippers soon underwent a process of "evolution," and was sub- jected to "transformation." It still retained in its new form its former weakness of religious thought and its narrow character of philosophic interests, its former *terre-à-terre* realism, but it completely lost its past truthfulness. The " house " now was termed "the Kingdom of God on Earth," and the "hole" received the name of " the new Gospel," whilst the distinction between the sham gospel and the true one (and this is the most distressing fact about it), a distinction which is exactly similar to that exist- ing between a hole drilled in a beam, and complete living tree—this essential distinction was either neglected or confused by the new evangelists.

Of course, I do not assert a direct historical or "genetic" connection between the original sect of hole-worshippers and the teaching of the sham Kingdom of God and the sham Gospel. Neither is it important for my object, which is only to show clearly the essential identity of the two "teachings" with that moral distinction which has been stated above.

[The identity here lies in the purely negative and void character of both "doctrines." It is true, the "educated" hole-worshippers do not call themselves by this name, but go under the name of Christians, and their teaching is also passed as the Gospel, but Christianity without Christ, and the Gospel, *i.e.,* the *"message of good,"* without the only good worth announcing, *viz.,* without the real resurrection to the fulness of blessed life—these are as much a hollow space as is the ordinary hole drilled in a peasant's house. There would not be any need to speak about this at all were it not for the fact that over the rationalist hole the Christian flag is flown, tempting and confusing many of the "little ones." When the people who believe and cautiously declare that Christ has become *obsolete* and has been *superseded*, or that He never existed at all, and that His life is a myth invented by Paul, at the same time persistently call themselves "true Christians" and screen their teaching of hollow space by distorted quotations from the Gospel, is well-nigh time to put aside our indifference to, and our condescending contempt for, their opinions. The moral atmosphere is contaminated with systematic falsehoods, so the public conscience loudly demands that the evil work should be branded by its real name. The true object of polemics would in this case be not *the confuting of sham religion but the showing up of the actual fraud.*

This fraud has no excuse. Between me, as the author of three books, banned by the ecclesi- astic censorship on the one side, and these publishers of numerous foreign books, pamphlets, and leaflets on the other side, the question of external obstacles for an unreserved frankness in these matters does not seriously arise. The restraints of religious freedom, existing in our country, cause the greatest pain to my heart, for I see and feel to what a great extent these external restrictions bring harm to and impose burdens not only on those whom they directly hit, but mainly on the cause of Christianity in Russia, consequently on the Russian nation, con- sequently, again, on the Russian State.

No external situation can prevent a man who is honestly convinced in his opinions, stating them fully. If it is impossible to do so at home, one can do it abroad, and no one has availed himself of this opportunity to a greater extent than the teachers of the sham Gospel have done when the matters con- cerned have been the *practical* questions of politics and religion. Whilst as regards the main, the essential question there is no need even to go abroad in order to refrain from insincerity and artifice : the Russian censorship never demands that anybody should pronounce opinions that he does not hold, to simulate a faith in things he does not believe in, or to love and revere what he despises and hates. To maintain an honest attitude towards the known his- torical Person and His Work, the preachers of hollowness had only one thing to do in Russia : they should merely have "ignored" Him. But here is the strange fact: in this matter these men refuse to avail themselves either of the freedom of silence which they enjoy at home or of the freedom of speech which they enjoy abroad. Both here and there they prefer to show their allegiance to the Gospel of Christ; both here and there they decline to reveal honestly their real attitude to the Founder of Christianity either by a resolute word or by an eloquent silence, *i.e.,* to show that He is entirely alien to them, is for no object required and is only a hindrance in their way.

From their point of view the things they preach are *of themselves* clear, desirable and salutary for everybody. Their " truth " is self-supporting, and if a certain historical person happens to agree with it, so much is it the better for him, though this fact does not endow him with any special authority in their eyes, particularly when it is remembered that this person had said and done many things which for these people are nothing but a "temptation" and "madness."

Even supposing that these moralists in their very human weakness feel an irresistible desire to sus- tain their beliefs as well as their own " reason " by some historical authority, why, I ask, do they not look in history for *another* who shall be a more suit- able representative? There has for a long time been one waiting for such recognition—the founder of the widely-popular religion of Buddhism. He did really preach what they required: non-resistance, impossibility, inactivity, sobriety, etc., and succeeded even *without a martyrdom* to "make a brilliant career" for his religion. The sacred books of the Buddhists do really proclaim *hollowness*, and to make them fully agree with the new teaching of the same matter they would require only a little sim- plification in detail. On the contrary, the Scriptures of the Jews and Christians are filled and permeated throughout by a positive spiritual message which denies both ancient and modern emptiness, so that to be able to fasten the teaching of this latter to any of the statements taken from the Gospel or the Pro- phets it is necessary, by hook or by crook, to tear away such a statement from its natural connection with the whole of the book and the context. Whereas, on the other hand, the Buddhist "suttee" supplies whole masses of suitable parables and legends, and there is nothing in those books inimical in spirit to the new teaching.

By substituting the hermit of the Sacciah tribe for the "rabbi from Galilee," the sham Christians would have lost nothing of importance, but would win something very valuable indeed, at least in my eyes — they would win the possibility of being, even while erring, honestly thinking and to an extent consistent. But they do not want this. . . .

The hollowness of the teaching of the new religion and its logical contradictions are too apparent, and in this matter I have been satisfied to give (in the Third Discussion) only a brief, though complete, statement of their pronouncements, obviously con- tradictory in themselves and hardly capable of tempting anybody outside the hopeless class of people typified by my Prince. Should I succeed in opening anybody's eyes to the other side of the question and making any deceived but living soul feel all the moral falsity of this death-spreading teaching taken in all its entirety, the polemical object of this book would be fully achieved.

I am firmly convinced, however, that the exposure of an untruth made without reservation, should it even fail to produce any beneficent effect, still remains, apart from the fulfilment of duty it in- volves for its author, a measure of spiritual sanita- tion in the life of society, and brings useful results both in the present and in the future.

Bound up with the polemical object of these dialogues I also pursue a positive aim: to present the question of the struggle against evil and of the meaning of history from three different standpoints. One of these is based on a religious conception of the everyday life, which is characteristic of past times, and is given much prominence in the First

Discussion in the speeches of *the General*. The other, representing the ideas of culture and progress as prevailing in our time, is expressed and defended by *the Politician*, particularly in the Second Discus- sion. Lastly, the third standpoint, which is abso- lutely religious and which will yet show its decisive value in the future, is indicated in the Third Dis- cussion in the speeches of *Mr. Z.* and in the story by Father Pansophius. Personally, I unreservedly accept the last point of view. But I fully recognise the relative truth contained in the two others, and for this reason could with equal fairness express the opposing arguments and statements of *the Politician* and *the General*. The higher absolute truth does not exclude or deny the preliminary con- ditions of its realisation, but justifies, appreciates, and sanctifies them. If from a certain point of view the world's history is God's judgment of the world— *die Weltgeschichte ist das Weltgericht*—this in- volves a long and complicated contest or litigation between the good and the evil historical forces, and this contest, to come to a final solution, must needs involve both a determined struggle for existence between those forces, and their greater inner, there- fore peaceful, development in the common forms of culture. For this reason the General and the Politician are both right in the light of the Higher truth, and I could with complete sincerity place myself in the position of the one or the other. It is only the power of evil itself that is absolutely wrong, but not such means of fighting it as the sword of the soldier or the pen of the diplomat. These *weapons* must be appraised at their actual usefulness in the given circumstances and that must be considered the better of the two whose use is more effective in upholding the cause of good. St. Alexis the metropolitan, when peacefully pleading for the Russian princes at the Tartar Horde, and St. Sergius when blessing the arms of Dmitrius of the Don against the same Horde both equally served one and the same cause of good—that finds its expression in many various forms and fashions.

These discussions about evil and the militant and the peaceful methods of combating it, had to be concluded with a definite statement of the last, the extremest manifestation of evil in history the picture of its short-lived triumph and its final destruction At first I treated this subject in the form of a dia- logue, as I had treated the other parts, and with a similar sprinkling of the jocular element. But friendly criticisms convinced me that this method of exposition was doubly unsuitable: firstly, because the interruptions and interpolations required by the form of dialogue tended to weaken the interest in the story; and, secondly, because the colloquial and particularly the jocular character of conversation did not accord with the religious importance of the subject. I recognised the justice of these criticisms and accordingly altered the form of the Third Dis- cussion, introducing in it the reading from a MS. left by a monk after his death, of an independent short story of the Anti-Christ." This story, which earlier formed the subject of a public lecture, created a good deal of bewilderment and confused comment on the platform and in the Press, the main reason for which appears to be very simple: the prevailing insufficient knowledge of the references to Anti- Christ contained in the Scriptures and in Church tradition. These give indications of all the main features of Anti-Christ such as the inner significance of Anti-Christ as a religious impostor, who obtains the title of the Son of God by "stealing" it, and not by spiritual self-sacrifice; his connection with a false prophet, wizard, who seduces people by means of real and false miracles; the obscure and peculiarly sinful origin of Anti-Christ himself, who secures is external position of a monarch of the world by the help of evil powers; lastly, the general develop- ment and the end of his activity. Other particulars, characteristic of Anti-Christ and his false prophet, may also be found in the same sources. We have there, for instance, bringing down fire from Heaven," murdering the two witnesses of Christ, exposure of their bodies in the streets of Jerusalem, and many others.* To connect the events with each other and to make the story more speaking several details had to be introduced, partly based on his- torical conjectures, and partly created by imagine- tion. On the details of the latter kind, such as the semi-psychic, semi-conjuring

AUTHOR'S PREFACE.

tricks of the great magician with subterranean voices, fireworks, etc., I placed, it hardly needs saying, very little import- ance, and I think was justified in expecting a similar attitude on the part of my "critics." As regards the other and extremely essential point the charac- teristics of the three impersonated confessions in the œcumenical council, this could be noticed and fully appreciated only by those of my critics who were acquainted with the history and life of the churches.

The character of the false prophet given in the Revelation and his mission, as clearly indicated therein, to mystify people for the benefit of Anti- Christ, made it necessary for me to attribute to him different prodigies of the kind that is peculiar to magicians and conjurers. It is known for certainty, *dass zein hauptwerk ein Feuerwerk sein wird*: " and he doeth great wonders, so that he maketh fire come down from heaven on the earth in the sight of men." Apocalypsis, xiii. 13.) At present we cannot, of course, know magic and mechanical technique of these prodigies, but we may be sure that in two or three centuries it will advance very far from what t is now, and what will be made possible by such progress for a magician like ours—is not for me to say. I have admitted to my story certain definite features and details only as concrete illustrations to the essential and fully-established relations, so that they would not be left mere bare schemes. The essential and the details should also be clearly dis- tinguished in all that I say about Pan-Mongolism and the Asiatic invasion of Europe. But, of course, the main fact itself has not in this case the absolute certainty which characterises the future coming and the fate of Anti-Christ and his false prophet. Nothing has been taken direct from the Scriptures in describing the development of the Mongolo- European relations, though a great deal of it can be based on Scriptural statements. Taken in general, the history indicated presents a series of conjec- tures of the probable based on the actual facts. Personally, I believe this probability to be very near the certainty, and this appears so, not only to me, but also to many much more important personages. For the sake of coherency of the story, several de- tails had to be introduced into these considerations of the coming Mongolian menace, for which I, of course, cannot vouch, and which, on the whole, were sparingly used. The thing of much greater import- ance to me was to make the picture of the coming terrific conflict of the two worlds as realistic as pos- sible, and to show thereby the pressing necessity of peace and true friendship amongst all the nations of Europe.

If the general cessation of war seems to me im- possible before the final catastrophe is over, I firmly believe that the closest friendship and peaceful co- operation of all the Christian nations and States is not only a possible but a necessary and morally imperative way for the salvation of the Christian world from being swallowed up by the lower elements.

So as not to make the story too long and too com- plicated I had to leave out another conjecture of mine which deserves a few words of explanation. It seems to me that the coming success of Pan- Mongolism will be greatly facilitated by the stub- born and exhaustive struggle which some of the European countries will have to wage against the awakened Islam in Western Asia and in the North and Central Africa. A greater part than it is generally believed will be played in that awakening by the secret and incessant activity of the religious and political brotherhood of "Senussi," which has for the movements of modern Mahomedanism the same directing importance as in the movements of the Buddhistic world belongs to the Tibetian brother- hood of "Kelani," in Lhasa, with all its Indian, Chinese, and Japanese ramifications. I am far from being absolutely hostile to Buddhism, neither am I particularly so to Islam. But a wilful blindness to the existing and coming state of things is too readily indulged in by many people to-day, and I might perhaps have chosen for myself a more profitable occupation.

The historical forces reigning over the masses of humanity will yet have to come to blows and become intermingled with each other before the new head grows on the self-lacerating body of the beast: the world-unifying power of the Anti-Christ, who "will speak high-sounding and splendid words," and will cast a glittering veil of good and truth over the mystery of utter lawlessness in the time of its final revelation, so that even the chosen, in the words of the Scriptures, will be reduced to the great be- trayal. To show be forehand this deceptive visor, was my highest aim in writing this book.

AUTHOR'S PREFACE.

Concluding, I must express my sincere gratitude to M. A. P. Salomon, who corrected and supple- mented my topographical data of modern Jerusalem; to M. N. A. Veliaminov, who communicated to me the story of the bashi-bazouk "kitchen," which he personally witnessed in 1877; and to M. M. Bibikov, who carefully examined the General's narrative in the First Discussion and pointed out some errors from the military standpoint, which have now been amended.

Even in this amended form, however, I still feel numerous defects of the work. But not less felt is also the distant image of pale death, which quietly advises me not to put off the publication of this book to an indefinite and little secure date. Shall I be given time for new works, I shall be given it for improving the old ones as well. If not—the statement of the coming historical issue of the moral struggle has been made by me in sufficiently clear, though brief, outlines, and I publish this little work with the grateful feeling of a fulfilled moral duty.

VLADIMIR SOLOVIEV.
Easter, 1900.

This preface was originally published in the newspaper, Russia, under the title "On the False Good." When preparing "The First Discussion" for publication as a separate volume, V. Soloviev made in the text numerous corrections. In a fateful manner, however, one of these corrections has proved unnecessary. On the advice of his friends he struck out the words which seemed to bear too personal a character, viz.: " but not less felt is also the distant image of pale death, which quietly advises me not to put off the publication, etc." These words, which were only too soon justified, should remain in the amended text as it stands now.

M. SOLOVIEV
(Editor of the Russian edition).

WAR, PROGRESS, AND THE END OF HISTORY

FIRST DISCUSSION

Audiatur et prima *pars*

THREE DISCUSSIONS

IN the garden of one of the villas that nestle together under the foothills of the Alps, and gaze into the azure depths of the Mediterranean, there happened to meet together this spring five Russians.

The first was an old GENERAL, a man of war from his youth. The second was a statesman, enjoying a hard-earned rest from the whirl and turmoil of politics—him I shall henceforth call the POLITICIAN. The third was a young PRINCE, whose strong democratic views and thirst for reform had led him to publish a large number of more or less valuable pamphlets on moral and social progress. The fourth was a middle-aged LADY, very inquisitive and greatly interested in humanity at large. And the last, another gentleman, of somewhat uncertain age and social position—whom we will call MR. Z.

At the frequent discussions which took place among them I myself was a silent listener. Certain of these discussions appeared to me to be particu- larly interesting; I therefore took care to write them down while they were still fresh in my mind. The first discussion was started in my absence and was provoked by some newspaper article or pamphlet on the literary campaign against war and military ser- vice, a campaign originated by Count Tolstoy and now being carried on by Baroness Zutner and Mr. Stead. The POLITICIAN, questioned by the LADY as to his opinion of this movement, characterised it as being well-intentioned and useful. This state-ment immediately called forth angry remarks from the GENERAL, who began to sneer at the leaders of this anti-war crusade, calling them ironically the true pillars of statesmanlike wisdom, the guiding stars on the political horizon, and dubbing them the three "whales" of the Russian land.[1] To this latter remark the POLITICIAN rejoined: "Well, there may be other *fishes* besides." This, for some reason, greatly delighted MR. Z., who, as he subsequently stated, made both opponents agree in regarding the whale as a fish. He even made them give a defini-tion of what a fish is, viz., an animal, belonging partly to the Admiralty and partly to the Depart-ment of Waterways. I think, however, that this is a pure invention of MR. Z. Be this as it may, I am unable to reconstruct the beginning of the dis-cussion in the proper manner, and as I do not venture to evolve it out of my inner consciousness, after the manner of Plato and his imitators, I commence my chronicle with the words uttered by the GENERAL, just as I joined the company.

---

[1] According to the Russian folklore the Earth rests on three whales. (Translator.)

THE FIRST DISCUSSION.

"Audiatur et **prima** *pars."*

GENERAL (*excited; speaks, incessantly getting up and sitting down, with many quick gesticulations*]. Oh, no! How is that? Oh, no! no! Answer me this one question: Does such a thing as a Christ-loving and glorious Russian Army truly exist at this moment? Yes or no?

POLITICIAN (*lounging comfortably in an easy- chair, and speaking in a tone suggestive of a compound of Epicurus, a Prussian colonel, and Voltaire*]. Does a Russian Army exist? Obviously it does. Why, you surely haven't heard that it had been abolished?

GENERAL. How mightily ingenuous you are to be sure! You understand perfectly well that that is not what I mean. I ask you this: Am I right in regarding our present Army as a glorious band of Christ-loving warriors, or am I to suppose that one ought to call it something else?

POLITICIAN. I see! That is what bothers you, is it? Well, you have brought your question to the wrong shop. You should inquire at the Department of Heraldry—they are the recognised experts in titles, I believe.

MR. Z. (*speaking as if he had an idea at the back of his mind*). And the Department of Heraldry will probably tell the General that the law places no restriction on the use of old titles. Did not the last Prince Lusignan hold the title of King of Cyprus, although he not only had no jurisdiction in Cyprus, but could not even drink Cyprian wine owing to his weak stomach and empty purse? Why, then, shouldn't the modern army be entitled a Christ-loving band of warriors?

GENERAL. Entitled! Then we may call black and white titles? So are sweet and bitter, and so are hero and scoundrel.

MR. Z. But I am not stating my own opinion. I merely put forward that which appears to be held by people who should know!

LADY (*to the Politician*). Why do you argue about mere forms of expression? I am sure the General has more to say about his " Christ-loving band of warriors."

GENERAL. I thank you, madam. What I wished, and what I still wish to say is this : From the earliest times until but yesterday every warrior, be he private or field-marshal, knew and felt that he served in a good and holy cause. He believed not only that he fulfilled duties every bit as necessary as sanitation or washing, for instance, but that he was part of a service which was good, honourable, and noble in the highest sense of the word, and to which the greatest and best men that have ever lived—heroes and leaders of nations—have given their lives. This cause of ours has always been sanctified and exalted by the Church, and glorified by the praise of the nation. Yet behold! one fine morning we are told that we must forget all this and that we must hold ourselves and our place in the world to be the very opposite. The cause which we have served, and always have been proud of serving, is suddenly declared to be a thing of evil and a menace to the country. Warfare, it appears, is against God's express commandments, is entirely opposed to human sentiments, and inevitably brings about most dreadful evil and dire misfortune. All nations, we are told, must combine against it and make its final destruction only a question of time.

PRINCE. Do you mean to tell us that you have ever before heard opinions which utterly condemn war and military service as relics of ancient barbarism?

GENERAL. Who has not? Of course I have heard them, and

have read them, too, in more languages than one! But all such puny voices—you must pardon my frankness—seem to me by no means the thunderclaps that you consider them. But to-day matters are different; one cannot but hear these opinions, expressed as they are on all sides. What on earth are we to do? Am I—and for that matter, every other soldier—to regard myself an honourable man, or an inhuman monster? Am I to respect myself as a willing servant in a noble cause, or am I to view my occupation with abhorrence, to repent of my misdeeds in sackcloth and ashes, and to ask pardon on my knees of every civilian for the sins of my profession?

POLITICIAN. What a fantastic way of stating the question! As if anybody were asking you anything extraordinary. The new demands are addressed, not to you, but to diplomatists and other "civilians" who care precious little whether soldiers are vicious or whether they are Christ-loving. As far as you yourself are concerned, there is only one thing to be done; and that is that you should carry out un- questioningly the orders of the authorities.

GENERAL. Well, well! As you take no interest in military matters it is only natural that your idea of them should be "fantastic," to use your own expression. You are obviously unaware that in certain cases the order of the authorities has no other meaning than that you must not wait or ask for their orders.

POLITICIAN. For instance?

GENERAL. For instance, just imagine that by the will of the powers that be I am placed in command of a whole military district. From this very fact it follows that I am commanded to govern and control in every way the troops placed in my charge. I am to develop and strengthen in them a definite point of view—to act in some definite way on their will—to influence their feelings; in a word, to educate them, so to speak, up to the purpose of their being. Very well then. For this purpose I am empowered, amongst other things, to issue to the troops of my district general orders in my name and on my entire personal responsibility. Well, should I apply to my superior officers, asking them to dictate to me my orders, or merely to instruct in what form they should be drawn up, don't you think I should, in return, be dubbed "an old fool"? And that if it happened again, I should be summarily dismissed? This means that I must adopt towards my troops a consistent policy, some definite spirit which, it is supposed, has been previously and once and for all approved and confirmed by the higher command. So that even to inquire about it would be to show either stupidity or impertinence. At present, how- ever, this "definite spirit," which, as a matter of fact, has been one and the same from the times of Sargon and Assurbanipal to those of William II.— this very spirit suddenly proves to be under sus- picion. Until yesterday I knew that I had to develop and strengthen in my troops not a new, but this same old *fighting* spirit—the willingness of each individual soldier to conquer the enemy or to go to his death. And for this it is absolutely necessary to possess an unshaken faith in war as a holy cause. But now this faith is being deprived of its spiritual basis, the military work is losing what the learned call" its moral and religious sanction."

POLITICIAN. How frightfully exaggerated all this is! There is no such radical change of views in reality. On the one hand, everybody has always recognised that war is evil and that the less there is of it the better. On the other hand, all serious people to-day realise that it is the kind of evil which it is impossible to eradicate completely at present. Consequently the question is not whether war can be abolished, but whether it can be gradually, even if very slowly, reduced to the narrowest limits. As to the attitude to war as a principle, this remains as it has ever been: it is an unavoidable evil, a misfortune, tolerable only in extreme cases.

GENERAL. And nothing else?

POLITICIAN. Nothing else.

GENERAL (*springing up from his seat*). Have you ever had occasion to refer to the Book of Saints?

POLITICIAN. You mean in the calendar? Oh, yes, I have sometimes to run through a long list of names of saints in order to find the dates of certain birth- days.

GENERAL. Did you notice what saints are men- tioned there?

POLITICIAN. There are different kinds of saints.

GENERAL. But what are their callings?

POLITICIAN. Their callings are as different as their names, I believe.

GENERAL. That is just where you are wrong. Their callings are not different.

POLITICIAN. What? Surely all the saints are not military men?

GENERAL. Not all, but half of them.

POLITICIAN. Exaggeration again!

GENERAL. We are not taking a census for statis- tical purposes here. What I maintain is that all the saints of our Russian church belong only to two classes: they are either monks of various orders, or princes—men who, from what we know of past history, must have been military men. And we have no other saints—I mean those of the male sex. Monk or warrior—that is all.

LADY. You forget the "innocents," don't you?

GENERAL. Not at all! But " innocents" are a kind of irregular monks, aren't they? What Cossacks are to the Army, "innocents" are to the "monkhood." This being so, if you now find me amongst the Russian saints a single clergyman, or tradesman, or deacon, or clerk, or commoner, or peasant—in a word, a man of any profession except monks and soldiers— then you may take the whole of my winnings which I may bring home from Monte Carlo next Sunday.

POLITICIAN. Thanks very much. Keep your treasures and your half of the book of saints—the whole of it, if you like. But do please explain what it is that you are trying to prove by this discovery of yours. Is it only that nobody but a monk or a soldier can set us a true example of moral life ?

GENERAL. That is hardly the point. I myself have known many highly virtuous persons amongst the clergy, the bankers, the official classes, and the peasants, but the most virtuous person I can recollect was the old nurse of one of my friends. But it is not about this that we are talking. I mentioned the saints only to point out that it could hardly have been possible for so many soldiers to become saints, side by side with monks and in preference to members of every other peaceful and civic profession, were military occupations always regarded as a necessary evil something like the liquor traffic or things even—worse. It is evident that the Christian nations, at whose instance the books of saints were actually compiled (and not only with the Russians was it so, but very much the same with other nations), not only respected the military calling, but they particularly respected it, and of all the lay profes- sions only the military one was held fit to contribute members to the saintship. It is this view which seems to be incompatible with the modern campaign against war.

POLITICIAN. But I did not say that there is no change whatever. Some desirable change is un- doubtedly taking place. It is true that the halo which crowned warriors and their wars in the eyes of the masses is fast disappearing. But matters have been tending this way for some long time. Besides, whose interests does this actually affect? Only that of the clergy, I should say, as the manu- facture of halos belongs exclusively to its depart- ment. It will, of course, be necessary to clear up some difficulties there. And what it will be im- possible to suppress will be interpreted symbolically, whilst the rest will wisely be kept quiet or relegated to oblivion.

PRINCE. These modifications are already being made. In connection with my publications I have to watch our ecclesiastical literature, and in two papers I had the pleasure of reading that Christianity absolutely condemns war.

GENERAL. Is that really so?

PRINCE. I could scarcely believe my own eyes myself. But I can show it.

POLITICIAN (*to the General*). You see! Why, though, should you be worried about it? Aren't you warriors men of deeds and not of windy words? Is all this merely professional selfishness and ambition on your part? If it is, it is indeed bad of you. But I repeat again: in practice everything remains for you as before. Let it be true that the system of militarism, which now for thirty years has been an insupportable burden to everybody, is now bound to disappear. However, an army of some size must still remain. And in so far as it will be admitted that it is necessary, just so far the same fighting qualities as before will be demanded of it.

GENERAL. That's it. You are all great masters to ask for milk from a dead bull! But who is to give you the required fighting qualities, when the first fighting quality, without which all others are of little use, is a cheerful and confident spirit, itself the outcome of faith in the sacredness of the cause to which one has devoted oneself? How then is this to happen, when it is recognised that war is crime and villainy, and that it is tolerated only in certain extreme cases as an unfortunate necessity?

POLITICIAN. Nobody expects this to be believed by military men. If they chose to regard themselves first men in the world, nobody would care a button about it. It was explained to you before, was it not, that Prince Lusignan is allowed to style himself the King of Cyprus, provided he does not ask us to give him money for Cyprian wine. So if you do not raid our pockets more than is necessary you may regard yourselves the salt of the earth and the flower of mankind nobody will stop you.

GENERAL. You say, regard yourselves! But, surely, we are not talking on the moon. Are you going to keep soldiers in a sort of vacuum, so that no foreign influences could reach them? And this in the days of universal military service, short period of training, and cheap Press! No, the matter is only too clear. When once military service is compulsory for all and everybody, and when once in the whole of society, from such representatives of the State as yourself, for example, to the lowest, the new adverse criticism of the military profession becomes uni- versally accepted, this view must needs be assimi- lated by the military men themselves. If all, from the higher command downwards, begin to regard military service as an evil, inevitable for *the present* then, in the first place, nobody will ever of his own accord choose the military calling for his life's work, with the exception perhaps of the dregs of society, which can find no other career open to it; and, secondly, all those who will be compelled to bear temporarily the military levy will do so with feelings similar to those with which criminals, chained to wheelbarrows, carry their fetters. Talk of fighting qualities and fighting spirit under such conditions! What drivel!

MR. Z. I have always believed that after the introduction of universal military service, the aboli- tion of armies, and eventually of individual States, is only a question of time, and that not far removed from the present moment, considering the rapid pro- gress of events.

GENERAL. Perhaps you are right.

PRINCE. I think that you are most certainly right, though the idea has never occurred to my mind in this guise. But it is splendid! Only think: militarism creates, as its most extreme expression, the system of universal service, and then, owing to this very fact, not only modern militarism, but the very foundations of the military system as such, become utterly destroyed. Isn't it wonderful!

LADY. Look! Even the Prince's face has brightened up. This is a pleasant change. The Prince hitherto has been wearing a gloomy counten- ance, which ill suited his profession of "true Christian."

PRINCE. One sees so many sad things around. There is but one joy left: the thought that reason will inevitably triumph in spite of all obstacles.

MR. Z. There can be no doubt that militarism in Western Europe and Russia is feeding upon itself. But as to the joys and triumphs which are to proceed from this fact—those yet remain to be seen.

PRINCE. What? You seem to doubt that war and militarism are absolute and utter evils, of which humanity must rid itself at any cost and immedi- ately? You doubt that complete and immediate suppression of this barbarism would in any *case* result in a triumph for reason and good?

MR. Z. I am positively certain of quite the *opposite*.

PRINCE. That is, of what?

MR. Z. Of the fact that war is not an absolute evil, and that peace is not an absolute good; or, putting it in a simpler way, that it is possible to have—and we do have sometimes—such a thing as *a good war*, and that it is also possible to have— and we do have sometimes—*an evil peace*.

PRINCE. Now I see the difference between your view and that held by the General: he believes, doesn't he, that war is always a good thing, and that peace is always a bad thing?

GENERAL. By no means! I understand perfectly well that sometimes war can be a very bad thing, as, for instance, was the case when we were beaten at Narva, or Austerlitz. And peace also can be a splendid thing, as, for example, the peace concluded at Nistaadt, or Kuchuk-Kainardji.

LADY. Is this a variant of the famous saying of a Kaffir or Hottentot, who told the missionary that he understood very well the difference between what is good and what is evil:—"Good is when I carry away somebody else's wives and cows, and evil is when mine are carried away from me"?

GENERAL. Don't you see that we, that is, I and your African, were only trying to say something witty: he was so unintentionally, I purposely. But now let us hear how clever people are going to discuss the question of war from the standpoint of morals.

POLITICIAN. I would only wish that our "clever people" would not land us in casuistry and metaphysics in discussing that perfectly clear and historically-limited problem.

PRINCE. Clear from what point of view?

POLITICIAN. My point of view is an ordinary one, a European one, which is being gradually assimilated by cultured people, even in other parts of the world.

PRINCE. And its essence is, of course, that every- thing is considered relatively and that no absolute difference is admitted between "must" and "must not," between good and evil. Isn't it so?

MR. Z. Pardon me. But this argument seems to me rather useless in relation to the problem we are discussing. To take myself as an instance, I fully recognise the absolute opposition between moral good and evil. At the same time, it is as perfectly clear to me that war and peace do not come within the scope of the argument; that it is quite impossible to paint war all solid black, and peace all pure white.

PRINCE. But this involves a contradiction. If the thing which is evil in itself, as, for instance, murder, can be good in certain cases, when you are pleased to call it war, what becomes then of the absolute difference between evil and good?

MR. Z. How simple it is for you! "Every kind of murder is absolute evil ; war is murder; it follows then that war is absolute evil." The syllogism is first rate! The only thing you lose sight of is that both your premises, the major and the minor, have first to be proved, and that consequently your con- clusion so far rests on air.

POLITICIAN. Didn't I tell you we should be landed in casuistry?

LADY. What is it they are talking about?

POLITICIAN. Oh, about some sort of major and minor premises.

MR. Z. Pardon me. We are coming to business presently. So you maintain that at any rate killing, that is taking somebody's life, is absolute evil, don't you?

PRINCE. Undoubtedly.

MR. Z. But to be killed—is this absolute evil or not?

PRINCE. From the Hottentot standpoint, of course it is. But we have been discussing moral evil, and this can exist only in the actions of an intelligent being, controlled by itself, and not in what happens to that being independently of its will. It follows that to be killed is the same as to die from cholera or influenza. Not only is it not absolute evil—it is not evil at all. Socrates and the stoics have already taught us this.

MR. Z. Well, I cannot answer for people so ancient as those. As to your moral appreciation of murder, this seems to limp somewhat. According to you it follows that absolute evil consists in causing a person something which is not evil at all. Think what you like, but there is something lame here. However, we will leave this lameness alone lest we really land in casuistry. To sum up, in killing, the evil is not in the physical fact of a life being taken, but in the moral cause of this fact, namely, in the evil will of the one who kills. Do you agree ?

PRINCE. It is so, of course. For without this evil will there is no murder, but only misfortune or in- advertence.

MR. Z. That is clear, when there is no will what- ever to murder, as, for instance, in the case of an unsuccessful operation. It is possible, however, to imagine a position altogether different: when the will, though not setting itself as an object the taking away of a human life, yet before the fact gives its consent to a murder, regarding it as an extreme and unavoidable measure. Would such a murder also be an absolute evil in your opinion?

PRINCE. Decidedly so, when once the will has agreed to a murder.

MR. Z. You will admit, however, that there are cases in which the will, though agreeing to a murder, is at the same time not an evil will. The murder is consequently not an absolute evil in that case, even when looked at from this subjective side?

PRINCE. Oh, dear me! This is something quite unintelligible. However, I think I guess what you mean: you refer to that famous case in which a father sees in a lonely place a blackguardly ruffian trying to assault his innocent (and, to enhance the effect, it is added his "little") daughter. The father, unable to protect her in any other way, kills the offender. I have heard this argument at least a thousand times.

MR. Z. What is really remarkable is not that you have heard it a thousand times, but the fact that nobody has ever had from any one of those holding your view a sensible, or even only plausible, answer to this simple argument.

PRINCE. And what is there in it to answer?

MR. Z. Well, if you don't like to argue against it, will you then prove by some direct and positive method that in all cases without exception, and con- sequently in the case we are discussing, it is indisput- ably better to abstain from resisting evil by means of force, than it is to use violence, though one risk the possibility of killing a wicked and dangerous man.

PRINCE. It is funny to ask for a *special* proof for a single case. Once you recognise that murdering generally is evil in the moral sense, it is clear that it will be evil in every single case as well.

LADY. This sounds weak, Prince, to be sure.

MR. Z. Very weak indeed, I should say. That it is *generally* better not to kill anybody than to kill is a truth which is not subject to argument and is accepted by everybody. It is just the single cases that actually raise the problem. The question is : Is the general and undisputable rule, " don't kill," unreservedly *absolute* and, therefore, admitting of *no* exception whatever, in no single case and in *no* circumstances; or is it such as to admit of even one exception, and, therefore, is not absolute ?

PRINCE. I cannot agree to such a formal way of approaching the problem. I don't see the use of it. Suppose I admit that in your exceptional case, purposely invented for argument's sake . . .

LADY (*reprovingly*). Prince! Prince! What is this I hear? . . .

GENERAL (*ironically*). Ho-ho-ho, Prince !

PRINCE (*taking no notice*). Let us admit that in your imaginary case to kill is better than not to kill (in point of fact, of course, I refuse to admit it), but let us take it for the moment that you are right. We may even take it that your case is not imaginary, but quite real, though, as you will agree, it is ex- tremely rare, exceptional. . . . But then we are dealing with war with something that is general, universal. You will not say yourselves that Napoleon, or Moltke, on Skobelev were in the position in any way resembling that of a father compelled to defend his innocent little daughter from the assaults of a monster.

LADY. That's better ! Bravo, *mon prince*!

MR. Z. A clever way, indeed, to avoid a difficult question. You will allow, me, however, to establish the connection, logical as well as historical, that exists between these two facts—the single murder and the war. For this let us take again your example, only we will strip it of the details which seem to increase, though actually they only diminish, its importance. We need not trouble ourselves about a father, or a little daughter, for with them the problem at once loses its pure ethical meaning, being transferred from the sphere of intellectual and moral consciousness into that of natural moral feelings : parental love will obviously make the father kill the villain on the spot, without any further consideration as to whether he must, or has the right to do so in the light of the higher moral ideal. So let us take not a father, but a childless moralist, before whose eyes some feeble being, strange and unfamiliar to him, is being fiercely assaulted by a cowardly villain. Would you suggest that the moralist should fold his arms and preach the glory of virtue while the fiendish beast is torturing his victim? Do you think the moralist will not feel a moral impulse to stop that beast by force, however great the possibility, or even the probability, of killing him may appear? And should he instead permit the dastardly deed to take place to the accompaniment of his high-sounding phrases, don't you think that he would find no rest from his conscience, and would feel ashamed of himself to the verge of repulsion?

PRINCE. Perhaps all that you are saying will be felt by a moralist who does not believe in the reality of the moral order, or who may have forgotten that God is not in might, but in right.

LADY. Very well said, Prince. Now, Mr. Z., what will you answer to this?

MR. Z. I will answer, that I wish it was even better said I mean more frankly, more simply, and more closely to the actual facts. You wanted to say, did you not, that a moralist who really believes in the justice of God must, without forcibly interfering with the villain, raise his prayers to God that He should prevent the evil deed being carried out : either by a moral miracle, by suddenly turning the villain to the path of truth; or by a physical miracle, by an instantaneous paralysis, say, or——

LADY. No special need for a paralysis; the mis- creant can be frightened by something, or in some other way prevented from carrying on his nefarious work.

MR. Z. Oh, well, that makes no difference. The miracle lies, you understand, not so much in the fact itself as in the connection of that fact be it a bodily paralysis or some mental excitement—with the prayer and its moral object. At any rate, the method suggested by the Prince is nothing else but a prayer for a miracle.

PRINCE. But . . . really . . . why a prayer . . . and a miracle?

MR. Z. What else is it then?

PRINCE. Well, if I believe that the world is governed by a beneficent and intelligent living Power, I cannot but also believe that whatever takes place in the world is in accord with that Power, that is, with the will of God.

MR. Z. Pardon me. How old are you?

PRINCE. Whatever do you mean by this question?

MR. Z. Nothing offensive, I can assure you. I presume you are not less than thirty, are you?

PRINCE. Guess higher!

MR. Z. So you must have assuredly had some occasion to see, or if not to see then to hear, or if not to hear then at least to read in the papers, that malicious and immoral things do happen in this world.

PRINCE. Well?

MR. Z. How is it then? Does it not prove that "the moral order/" or the will of God, obviously does not manifest itself in the world by its own power?

POLITICIAN. Now we are at last getting to busi- ness. If evil exists, the gods, it follows, either cannot or will not suppress it, and in both cases the gods, as omnipotent and beneficent powers, do not exist at all. 'Tis old but true!

LADY. Oh, what awful things you are saying!

GENERAL. Talking does lead one to great dis- coveries. Only begin philosophising, and your feeble brain reels.

PRINCE. A poor philosophy this! As if the will of God were bound up with our ideas of what is good and evil.

MR. Z. With *some* of our ideas it is not, but with the true notion of good it is bound up most firmly. Otherwise, if God is generally indifferent to good and evil, you then utterly refute your own argument.

PRINCE. How is that, I should like to know?

MR. Z. Well, if you hold that God is not con- cerned when a powerful blackguard, swayed by his brute passions, crushes a poor feeble creature, then God is even more likely to have no objection if any one of us, actuated by human sympathy, crushes the blackguard. You will surely not attempt to defend the absurdity that only killing a weak and inoffensive being *is not* evil before the eyes of God, whereas killing a strong and wicked beast is evil.

PRINCE. It appears to you as an absurdity only because you look at it from the wrong point of view. From the moral standpoint the real importance attaches not to one who is killed, but to one who kills. Just now you yourself called the blackguard a beast, that is, a being lacking in intelligence and conscience. If so, what evil can there be in his actions?

LADY. But don't you see that it is not a beast in the literal sense of the word as used here? As if I were to say to my daughter: " What nonsense you are talking, my angel," and you were to get up and begin shouting at me: "How ridiculous a thing to say ! How can angels talk nonsense? " Well, of all the arguments ! . . .

PRINCE. I crave your forgiveness. I understand perfectly well that the villain is called a beast only in a metaphorical sense, and that this beast has neither tail nor hoofs. But it is evident that the lack of intelligence and conscience is referred to here in its literal meaning; for it would be impos- sible for a man with intelligence and conscience to commit such acts.

MR. Z. Yet another play on words! Naturally, a man acting as a beast loses his intelligence and conscience in the sense that he is no longer moved by them. But that intelligence and conscience do not speak within him at all you still have to prove. In the meanwhile, I continue to think that a bestial man differs from me and you not by the absence of intelligence and conscience, but only by his willing- ness to act against them, and in accord with the im- pulse of the beast within him. Within every one of us lurks the beast, but we usually keep him tightly chained ; whilst the other man loosens the chain, only to be dragged along at the tail of the beast. He has the chain, but fails to make proper use of it.

GENERAL. Precisely. And if the Prince still dis- agrees with you he is hoist with his own petard! "The villain," the Prince says, "is only a beast without intelligence and conscience." Then killing him is the same as killing a wolf, or a tiger spring- ing at a man. Why, this sort of thing is permitted even by the Society for Prevention of Cruelty to Animals !

PRINCE. But you forget again that whatever the state of mind of that man may be, whether it be completely devoid of intelligence and conscience, or whether it be consciously and wilfully immoral, if such is possible, it is not he who really matters, but you; *your* intelligence and conscience are not destroyed and *you* do not want consciously to go against their demands—well then, you would not kill that man, whatever he might have been.

MR. Z. Naturally, I would not kill him, should my intelligence and conscience absolutely forbid my doing so. Imagine, however, that intelligence and conscience tell me something entirely different—something which seems to be more sensible and morally correct.

PRINCE. This sounds interesting! Let us hear it.

MR. Z. We may assume first of all that intelli- gence and conscience know how to count, at least, up to three . . .

GENERAL. Go on, go on!

MR. Z. Therefore intelligence and conscience, if they do not wish to lie to me, will not keep on telling me "two" when the actual number is "three" . . .

GENERAL (*impatiently*). Well?

PRINCE. I can't see what he is driving at!

MR. Z. Well, don't you assert that intelligence and conscience speak to me only about myself and the villain? The whole matter, according to your argument, is that I should not lay a finger on him. But in point of fact there is present also a third

Person—who is actually the most important of all— the victim of the wicked assault, who requires my help. You wilfully neglect her, but conscience speaks of her too, and of her even in preference to the others. And if the will of God is involved here at all, it is only in the sense that I should save the victim, sparing the villain as much as possible. But help her I must at any cost and in any case—by persuasion, if it be possible ; if not by force. And should my hands be tied, then and only then can I call to my aid that supreme resource which was sug- gested by you too prematurely and then too lightly cast aside—the supreme resource of Prayer, that is, by an appeal to the Divine Intelligence, which, I am sure, can really perform miracles when they are necessary. Which of these means of help should be used depends entirely on the internal and external conditions of the incident. The only absolute thing here is, that I must help those who are wronged. This is what my conscience says.

GENERAL. The enemy's centre is broken through! Hurrah!

PRINCE. My conscience has progressed beyond this elementary stage. My conscience tells me in a case like this something more definite and concise: "Don't kill!" it says, and that is all. However, I can't see even now that we have moved any farther in our argument. Suppose I agree with your proposi- tion that *everybody*, even a morally cultured and truly conscientious man, could permit himself to commit a murder, acting under the influence of sym- pathy and having no time to consider the moral character of his action—even admitting all this, I am still utterly unable to see what could follow from this admission that would enlighten us with regard to our principal problem. Let me ask you again: "Did Tamerlane, or Alexander the Great, or Lord Kitchener kill and make others kill people in order to protect weak, defenceless beings from the vil- lainous assaults that were threatening them?"

MR. Z. The juxtaposition of Tamerlane and Alexander the Great augurs ill for our historical accuracy, but as this is the second time that you have appealed to historical facts, allow me to quote from history an illustration which will really help us to compare the question of the defence of a person with that of the defence of a State. The affair hap- pened in the twelfth century, at Kiev. The feuda- tory princes, who as early as that seemed to hold your ideas on war and believed that one may quarrel and fight only "chez soi," would not agree to take the field against the Polovtziens, saying that they were reluctant to subject their people to the horrors of war. To this the great Prince Vladimir Mono- mach answered in the following words: " You pity the serf, but you forget that when spring comes the serf will go out to the field." . . .

LADY. Please don't use bad words!

MR. Z. But this is from a chronicle.

LADY. That makes no difference. I am sure you don't remember the chronicle by heart, so may just as well put it in your own words. It sounds so absurd. One hears " Spring will come" and expects "the flowers will blossom and the nightingales will sing," but instead all of a sudden comes " serf." [2]

MR. Z. As you please, madam. "The spring will come, the peasant will go out into the field with his horse to till the land. The Polovtzien will come, will kill the peasant, will take away his horse. Then a formidable band of Polovtziens will make an inroad, will slaughter all the men, capture their wives and children, drive away their cattle, and burn out their homes. Can't you find it in your heart to pity the peasants for this? I do pity them, and for that reason I call upon you to take up arms against the Polovtziens." The princes, ashamed of themselves, listened to his words, and the country enjoyed peace throughout the reign of Vladimir Monomach. Afterwards, however, they turned back to their "peaceful professions," which urged them to evade war with foreign enemies in order that they could carry on in comfort their miserable quarrels in their own homes. The end of it all for Russia was the Mongolian yoke, and for the descendants of these princes that rich feast of experience which history provided them in the person of Ivan the Terrible.

PRINCE. Your argument is absolutely beyond me!

At one moment you describe an incident which has never happened to any one of us, and will certainly never occur in the future. At another moment you remind us of some Vladimir Monomach, who per- haps never existed, and who, at any rate, has absolutely nothing to do with us. . . .

LADY. *Parlez pour vous, monsieur*!

MR. Z. Tell me, Prince, are you a descendant of Rurik?

---

[2] The equivalent Russian word "smerd" (serf, slave, &c.) suggests something stinking. (Translator.)

PRINCE. People say so. But do you suggest that I should for this reason take special interest in Rurik, Sineus, and Truvor?[3]

LADY. I think when one does not know one's ancestors one is little better than the little boys and girls who believe that they were found in the garden under a cabbage-leaf.

PRINCE. And what are those poor devils to do who have no ancestors?

MR. Z. Everybody has at least two great ances- tors, who have bequeathed to posterity their circum- stantial and highly instructive records: the history of one's country and that of the world.

PRINCE. But these records cannot decide for us how we should live now, and what we should now do. Let it be granted that Vladimir Monomach actually existed, that he was not merely the creation of the imagination of the monk Laurentius, or the monk Hypathius. He may even have been an

GENERAL. Now that you reduce it all to personal conscience, allow me to tell you this much. I am a man who is in the moral sense (as in the other, of course) of the average type: neither black nor white, but grey. I have never been guilty either of any extraordinary virtue or of any extraordinary villainy. Even when one performs good acts there is always ground for self-suspicion. One can never say with certainty and with candour what one's real motive is. There may be a real good

---

[3] The legendary founders of the Russian State. (Trans- lator.) exceptionally good man, and may have sincerely pitied the "serf." In such case he was right in righting the Polovtziens, because in those barbaric times the moral consciousness had not yet risen above the crude Byzantine notion of Christianity, and actually approved of man-killing when it was for a good purpose, real or imaginary. But how can we do so, when we have once understood that murder is an evil thing, opposed to the will of God and forbidden since the days of Moses by God's commandment? Under no guise and under no name can killing ever become permissible for us. Still less can it cease to be evil when, instead of one man, thousands of people are slaughtered under the name of war. The whole thing is, in the first instance, a question of personal conscience.

or only a weakness of the soul, perhaps a habit of life, or sometimes even a personal vanity. Besides, this is all so petty. In all my life there was only one incident which I could not call "petty" to begin with, but, what is more important, in which I am certain I was not guided by any doubtful motive but solely by the impulse of good that overcame me. Only once in my life did I experience a complete moral satisfac- tion and even some kind of ecstasy, so that my actions were entirely free from considerations or hesitations. And this good act of mine has been to me till now, and will, of course, remain so for ever, my very best and purest memory. Well, this single good act of mine was a murder, and not a little insignificant murder at that, for in some quarter of an hour I killed over a thousand men!

LADY. *Quelles blagues!* And I thought you were quite serious for once!

GENERAL. And so I am. I can produce witnesses if you like. It was not with my own sinful hands that I killed, but with six pure, chaste steel guns, which poured forth a most virtuous and beneficent rain of shells.

LADY. Where was the good in that, I should like to know?

GENERAL. Though I am not only a soldier, but in modern parlance a "militarist," it is needless to say that I would not call the mere annihilation of a thousand ordinary men a good act, were they Germans, or Hungarians, or Englishmen, or Turks. Here it was quite an exceptional case. Even now I cannot speak calmly about it, so painfully it stirred my soul.

LADY. Please do not keep us on tenterhooks. Tell us all about it.

GENERAL. I mentioned guns. You will then have guessed that the affair happened in the last Russo-Turkish war. I was with the Caucasian army. After October 3rd . . .

LADY. What about October 3rd?

GENERAL. That was the day of the great battle in the Aladja mountains, when for the first time we crushed all the ribs of the "invincible" Hasi- Moukhtar Pasha. So after October 3rd we at once advanced into Asiatic country. I was on the left front at the head of the advance guard engaged in scouting. I had under me the Nijny-Novgorod dragoons, three "hundreds" of Kuban Cossacks, and a battery of horse artillery. The country was not particularly inspiring: in the mountains it was fairly decent, sometimes even beautiful. But down in the valleys nothing but deserted, burnt-out vil- lages and downtrodden fields were to be seen. One morning—October the 28th, it was—we were descending a valley, where according to the map there was a big Armenian village. As a matter of fact there was no village to be seen, though there had really been one there not long before, and of a decent size, too: its smoke could be seen miles away. I had my detachment well together in close formation, for reports had been received that we might run into a strong cavalry force. I was riding with the dragoons; the Cossacks were in advance.

There was a sharp bend in the road as we neared the village. Suddenly the Cossacks reined in their horses and stood as if they were rooted to the spot. I galloped forward. Before I could see anything I guessed by the smell of roasting flesh that the bashi-bazouks had left their "kitchen" behind. A huge caravan of Armenian refugees had not been able to escape in time. The crowd had been caught by the Turks, who had "made a good job of it" in their own inimitable fashion. They had bound the poor Armenians, some by the head, some by the feet, some by the waist, to the high cart axles, had lit fires underneath, and had slowly grilled them. Dead women lay here and there—some with breasts cut off, others with abdomens ripped open. I need not go into further particulars. But one scene will remain for ever vivid in my memory. A poor woman lay there on the ground, her head and shoulders securely bound to the cart's axle, so that she could not move her head. She bore no burns, no wounds. But on her distorted face was stamped a ghastly terror—she had evidently died of sheer horror. And before her dead, staring eyes was a high pole, firmly fixed in the ground, and to it was tied the poor little naked body of a baby—her son, most likely—a blackened, scorched little corpse, with eyes that pro- truded. Near by also was a grating in which lay the dead ashes of a fire. . . . I was completely overcome with the ghastliness of the thing.

In face of such revolting evidence I could not reason—my actions became mechanical. Grimly I bade my men put their horses to the gallop. We entered the burned village; it was razed to the ground; not a house remained. Presently we saw a poor wretch crawling out of a dry well. He was covered with mud; his clothes were in rags. He fell on his knees, and began wailing something in Armenian. We helped him to his feet, and plied him with eager questions. He proved to be an Armenian from a distant village, a fairly intelligent fellow. He had come to the place on business just as the inhabitants had decided to flee. They had hardly started off when the bashi-bazouks fell upon them — an immense number, he said—at least forty thousand. He managed to hide himself in the well. He heard the cries of the tortured people; he knew full well what was happening. Later, he heard the bashi-bazouks come back and go off again by a different route. "They were going to my own village," he groaned, "and then they will do the same terrible things to all our folk." The poor wretch moaned pitifully, wringing his hands in despair. At that moment an inspiration seemed suddenly to come to me. My agony of soul seemed suddenly comforted. This world of ours as sud- denly became once more a happy place to dwell in. I quietly asked the Armenian how long it was since those devils had left the place. He reckoned it about three hours.

" And how long would it take for a horse to get to your village?"

"Over five hours."

No, it was impossible to overtake them in two hours. What a damnable business!

"Do you know of another and shorter way to your place?" I asked.

"I do, sir, I do." And he became at once excited. "There is a way across the defile. It is very short. And only very few people know it."

"Is it passable on horseback ? "

"It is, sir."

"And for artillery?"

"It would be rather difficult, but it could be done, sir."

I ordered my men to supply the Armenian with a horse, and with all my detachment followed him into the defile. How we all seemed to crawl there among the mountains; yet I hardly seemed to notice anything by the way. Once more my actions had become merely mechanical. But in the depths of my soul I felt utter and complete confidence. I knew what I had to do, and I knew that it would be done. My heart was light; I trod on air; I exulted in the certain fulfilment of my plans.

We were already filing out from the last defile, after which we should come to the high road, when I saw our Armenian galloping back and waving his hands frantically, as if to say, " Here they are!" I caught up with the advance guard, and levelling my telescope I could see that he was right. I saw an apparently endless column of horses not forty thousand, of course, but three or four thousand at least, if not even five. These sons of devils at once spotted the Cossacks and turned to meet them. We were coming out of the defile against their left front. A hail of bullets greeted the Cossacks. These Asiatic monsters could fire their European guns as if they were really human beings. Here and there a Cossack was picked off by a shot. A Cossack officer rode up to me and shouted: "Order the attack, sir. Why should these beasts be allowed to shoot us like quails, while we are mounting our artillery? We can put them to flight ourselves."

"Patience, my dear fellow, for just one little moment," I told him. "I have no doubt that you would be able to put them to flight; but what would be the pleasure of that? God bids me wipe them out and not drive them away." Here I ordered two "hundreds" of Cossacks advancing in open order to let fly at the devils, and later, when well in the thick of it, to retreat on the battery. One hundred Cossacks I left to mask the guns, while the Nijny-Novgorod men were placed in phalanx to the left of the battery. I trembled with impatience. The murdered child with its staring, anguished eyes came vividly before me. The Cossacks were falling, shot! God! what an agony of suspense. . . .

LADY. And the end?

GENERAL. The end came just as I knew it must.

The Cossacks engaging the enemy presently began their retreat, yelling wildly in their usual fashion. Those sons of devils came pell-mell after them, too excited even to fire, and galloping *en masse* on our position. Within four hundred yards of our line the Cossacks suddenly scattered, each man seeking cover where he could. "At last," I felt, "God's hour has struck! " I turned to the squad of Cossacks covering the guns. "Cossacks! wheel! " I shouted. The covering squad divided, right and left, leaving the battery unmasked. One fierce prayer to God, and then I gave the word "Fire! "

And God heard me. He blessed fully and com- pletely every one of my six charges. Never in my life have I heard such a devilish yell. The swine did not come to their senses even when the second volley of shells smote them, cutting red lanes through and through.

Suddenly the horde wheeled. A third volley fol- lowed them up! What a bloody mess it made ! Have you seen an ants' nest, on which burning matches have been thrown?—the ants all rushing about, crushing each other? . . . In a moment our Cos- sacks and Dragoons had charged them on the left flank, cutting, hacking, and slicing them like cabbage. Few of them managed to get away: those who escaped the rain of shells were cut down by the sabres. Some threw their guns away, jumped off their horses, and whined for mercy. But I was past giving orders. My men understood well enough that it was not a time for mercy. So the Cossacks and the men of Nijny-Novgorod sabred them to a man.

It is a sure thing, however, that if these brainless Satans, after the first two volleys were fired point- blank into their midst at a range of about 40 to 60 yards, instead of rushing back had galloped on the battery, there would have been an end to all of us no third volley would have been fired. . . . Well, God was with us. The whole thing was over. And in my soul I felt the joy and peace of an Easter Sunday! We gathered our slain—thirty-seven good men they were—laid them together on the level ground in rows, and closed their eyes. I had an old sergeant in the third hundred, Odarchenko by name, an earnest student of the Bible and singularly gifted. In England he would have become a Prime Minister, I am sure. Now he is in Siberia, banished there for resisting the authorities when they were shutting up some "old-believers' " monastery and destroying the tomb of one of their sainted elders. I called him. "Well, Odarchenko," I said, " now that we are in the field there is no time for arguing about the 'hallelujahs,' so you be our priest and perform the funeral service over our dead." For him this was, of course, a Heaven-sent opportunity. "I shall be only too glad to do it, sir," he replied, and the face of the little beast fairly beamed with joy. There was also a rough-and-ready choir. The ser- vice was performed with all ceremony. Only the absolution was lacking, but this was not necessary either : their sins were already remitted by the words of Christ himself about those who "lay down their lives for their friends." Even now I can see the ceremony vividly before my eyes. The day had been cloudy, as it usually is in the autumn season, but at that moment the sky was clearing before the setting sun, and above the dark loom of the gloomy defile rose and amber-tinted clouds were gathering like God's own regiments. My soul was still in ecstasy with the glory of our fight. Wondrous peace rested upon me; I felt that all worldly stains were washed away, and that all the burden of earthly trouble had fallen from my shoulders. I was in Paradise—I was feeling God, and there was the end of it. And when Odarchenko started calling out the names of the departed warriors who on the battlefield had laid down their lives for their faith, their Tsar, and their country, I truly felt that verily there was such a thing as a Christ-loving band of warriors, and that it was no mere official expression, no mere empty title, as you were pleased to call it. I felt that war, as it was then, is now, and ever will be till the ending of the world, was something great, honourable, and holy. . . .

PRINCE (*after a short interval of silence*). Well, when you buried your men in your happy frame of mind, tell me, didn't you think at all of the enemies whom you had killed in such great numbers?

GENERAL. Thank God, we were able to move further before that carrion had time to remind us of itself.

LADY. Ah, now you have spoiled the whole im- pression. What a shame !

GENERAL (*addressing the Prince*). And what would you have me do? That I should give Christian burial to those jackals, who were neither Christians nor Moslems, but the Devil knows what ? Imagine for a moment that I went out of my senses and ordered the service to be performed over them, together with the Cossacks. Would not you in that case charge me with intolerance? To think of it! These poor dear fellows, when alive, worshipped the Devil and prayed to the fire, and now after their death they are suddenly to be subjected to superstitious and crude pseudo-Christian rites! No, I had something else then to worry about. I called all the officers and ordered them to tell the men that not one of them should dare to come within ten yards of the damned carrion. I could well see that my Cossacks' fingers itched to search the pockets of the killed, as was their habit. And who knows what plague they might have spread as a result? Let the Devil take the lot of it.

PRINCE. Do I understand you correctly? You were afraid lest the Cossacks should begin robbing the dead bashi-bazouks and should carry from them some infectious disease to your force?

GENERAL. That is exactly what I feared. I think the point is clear enough.

PRINCE. What a Christ-loving band of warriors!

GENERAL. Who, the Cossacks? They are veritable brigands! They were always like this.

PRINCE. But, really, what is all this? Are we talking in dreams?

GENERAL. It seems to me that there must be some- thing wrong. I can't make out what it is that you really want to know.

POLITICIAN. The Prince is probably surprised that your ideal and all but canonised Cossacks all of a sudden prove, in your own words, to be utter brigands!

PRINCE. That's it. And I ask you, how can war be "something great, honourable, and holy," when you admit yourself that it is a struggle between one group of brigands and another?

GENERAL. Now I see your point. "A struggle of one group of brigands with another." But don't you see that the *others* are of quite a different sort? Or do you really believe that to rob when occasion offers itself is the same as to roast little babies before the eyes of their mothers? Well, I'll tell you this much. So clear is my conscience in this matter that even now I sometimes regret with all my soul that I did not die after I had given the order to fire the last volley. I have not the slightest doubt that should I have died then, I should have gone before the Throne of God with all my thirty-seven slain Cossacks, and we would have taken our places in Paradise by the side of the Penitent Thief. It was not for nothing that the Bible placed him there, was it?

PRINCE. That is true. But you will certainly not find it written in the Bible that only people of our own country or of our own religion can be likened to the Penitent Thief, and not people of all nation- alities and creeds.

GENERAL. Upon my word, you could not place more misstatements to my credit if I were already dead! When have I made distinctions among nations and creeds? Are Armenians my country- men and co-religionists? Or have I referred to the faith and nationality of that Devil's spawn which I annihilated by shells?

PRINCE. But you fail to remember the fact that the aforesaid Devil's spawn are, after all, human beings, that in every man you can find both good and evil, and that every brigand, be he a Cossack or a bashi-bazouk, might prove to be a "penitent thief."

GENERAL. How am I to take you? At one moment you say that an evil man is like an irre- sponsible beast, at another moment you state that a bashi-bazouk roasting babies might well prove to be a penitent thief. And all because you fear to touch evil even with one finger! To me the important point, however, is not that every man has within him the seeds of both good and evil, but as to which of the two—good or evil—has taken firmer root in him. It matters little that wine and vinegar are both made from the juice of the grape. What is of real importance is whether a certain bottle has wine or vinegar in it. Because, should it be vinegar and I begin drinking it glass after glass, and treat others to it simply because it happens to be made from the same material as wine, I am pretty certain that this exhibition of my cleverness will do nobody any good at all. On the contrary, it may ruin good digestions! Now, all men are brothers. Very good. I am glad to hear it. But how far will this take us? There are different kinds of brothers, you know. Why should I then not be inquisitive enough to find out which of my brothers is

Cain and which is Abel? And suppose I happen to see my brother Cain flaying my brother Abel, and because all men are brothers I deal out such a blow to my brother Cain as will teach him to give up for ever his bad habits, then you come out and blame me for forgetting that all three of us are brothers. Of course, I don't forget it. Why, it is only because I remember this brotherhood that I interfere at all. Otherwise I could pass by and take no notice.

PRINCE. But why those alternatives—either pass-ing by or dealing a blow?

GENERAL. No third issue can generally be found in such cases. You have been suggesting praying to God that He should personally interfere and by the might of His own right hand bring every Devil's son to his senses. But you yourself cast this idea aside, didn't you? I admit willingly that prayer is good in all circumstances, but it cannot be substituted for action on one's own part. Pious people, for instance, say prayers even before they have their meals, but they have to do their chewing themselves, and with their own jaws. Nor did I give orders to my horse artillery without saying my prayers!

PRINCE. Such prayers are blasphemy, of course. It is not praying to God that is necessary, but acting according to God's will.

GENERAL. For example?

PRINCE. A man who is imbued with the true Christian spirit will, in the hour of need, find within himself the power to influence a poor ignorant brother who is about to commit a murder or some other evil. By means of words and gestures, and even by his very looks, he will be able to make such a startling impression upon the mind of the wrongdoer that he will instantly see his error and will forsake the ways of evil.

GENERAL. Holy saints! Is it before the bashi-bazouks, who roasted babies, that you think I should have performed all those touching gestures and said these moving words?

MR. Z. Words, perhaps, would not have been quite opportune owing to the distance intervening and to the fact that neither of you understood the other's language. And as to gestures making a startling impression say what you will, nothing could have been more fitting in the circumstances than the rounds of shells fired.

LADY. Really, in what language and with the help of what instruments could the General make himself understood by the bashi-bazouks?

PRINCE. I have never said that the *General* could have impressed the bashi-bazouks in the Christian way. What I did say was that a man full of the true Christian spirit would have found some means, in this case as in every other, to awaken in those dark souls the good which lies hidden in every human being.

MR. Z. Do you really believe in this?

PRINCE. I have not the slightest doubt about it.

MR. Z. Well, do you think, then, that Christ was *sufficiently* imbued with this spirit?

PRINCE. What a strange question to ask!

MR. Z. I ask it only to learn from you why it was that Christ could not use the power of His spirit to such effect as to awaken the good hidden in the souls of Judas, Herod, the priests of the Sanhedrim, and, lastly, of that *impenitent* thief, who usually remains entirely forgotten when his penitent comrade is mentioned. There is no insuperable difficulty here for positive Christian thought. But you are obliged to sacrifice one of the two things: either your habit of quoting Christ and the Bible as the highest authority, or your moral optimism. Because, the third resource, which has been rather too much hackneyed—that of denying the very facts of the New Testament as a later invention or a mere priestly commentary—in the present case is entirely taken from you. However much you mutilate and sub-edit the text of the four Gospels to suit your object, what is the principal thing with us in our argument will remain in it indisputably, namely, that Christ suffered cruel persecutions and the tor- tures of crucifixion at the hands of malicious enemies. That personally He remained morally above all this spite, that He did not want to resist his enemies but forgave them—all this is equally easy to understand, both from my point of view and from yours. But why is it, then, that, forgiving His enemies, He— to use your own words—"did not save their souls" from the cloud of ignorance in which they were enwrapped? Why didn't He conquer their spite by the power of His benignity? Why didn't He awaken the good that lay dormant in them, and give enlightenment and new life to their souls? In short, why didn't He impress Judas, Herod, and the Sanhedrim in the same way in which He impressed the single penitent thief? It follows that: either He could not, or did not wish to do so. In both cases, however, according to your argument, Christ must have been insufficiently imbued with the true Christian spirit! On which conclusion I beg you to accept my hearty congratulations.

PRINCE. Oh! I refuse to fence with you in a duel of words, just as I refused to engage in combat with the General, using for weapons his " Christ- loving" swords. . . .

(Here the Prince stood up, evidently on the -point of saying something strong enough to flatten his opponent at a blow, and without fencing at all; but the bells of a neighbouring church struck the hour of seven.)

LADY. 'Tis time to have dinner. But a discus- sion like this should not be finished hurriedly. After dinner we play whist, but to-morrow this conversa- tion must certainly be continued. *(Addressing the Politician)* Do you agree?

POLITICIAN. To the continuation of this discus- sion? I am only too glad it has come to an end! Don't you think the argument has acquired much of the unpleasant quality of religious controversy? That is, I must say, altogether beyond justification. Besides, my life is the most precious thing to me.

LADY. It is no good pretending. You must, you must take part in the rest of the discussion. You ought to be ashamed of yourself—a Mephistopheles in secret, sprawling luxuriously on a sofa!

POLITICIAN. Very well, then. I have no objection to resuming the discussion to-morrow, but only on condition that religion is kept out of it as much as possible. I do not demand that it should be banished altogether—that seems to be impossible. But, for God's sake, let us have as little of it as we can.

LADY. Your "for God's sake" is very sweet in this connection.

MR. Z. (*to the Politician*). I think the best way to have as little religion as possible would be for you to monopolise the conversation!

POLITICIAN. I will, I promise you, although it is always more pleasant to listen than to speak, par- ticularly in this "salubrious air." But to save our little company from the contentious struggle which may perniciously reflect upon the whist too, I am willing to sacrifice myself for two hours.

LADY. How delightful of you! And on the day after to-morrow we will have the rest of our discus- sion on the Bible. The Prince will by that time prepare some absolutely irrefutable argument. But you must be ready too. After all, one should learn at least a little of matters ecclesiastical!

POLITICIAN. The day after to-morrow too? Oh, no! my self-sacrifice does not go so far as that! Besides, I have to go to Nice on that day.

LADY. To Nice? What a transparent pretext! It is useless, I assure you, for we saw through you long ago. Everybody knows that when a man says, "I have an appointment in Nice," he really proposes a bit of fun at Monte Carlo. Well, let it be so. After to-morrow we must manage somehow to do without you. Plunge yourself to the neck into pleasure—that is, if you are not afraid of becoming soon a ghost yourself. Go to Monte Carlo. And may Providence reward you according to your deserts.

POLITICIAN. My deserts do not concern *Provi- dence*, but only the *provision* of certain necessary measures I have carried out for the benefit of society. But I admit the influence of luck and the value of a little calculation in roulette as well as in everything else.

LADY. To-morrow, however, we all must meet here without fail.

SECOND DISCUSSION

Audiatur et secunda *pars*

THE SECOND DISCUSSION.

Audiatur et **secunda** *pars*

NEXT afternoon, at the appointed hour, we were having tea under the palm trees. Only the Prince was late; we had to wait for him. As I did not play cards that evening, I was able to take down the whole of the second discussion from the beginning. This time the Politician said so much, drawling out his interminable and intricate sentences in such a manner that I found it impossible for me to write down his exact words. I quote verbatim a fair amount, however, of what he said, and make some attempt to preserve his characteristic utterance; but more often I shall be found to give only the substance of his speech in my own words.

POLITICIAN. For some time now I have been observing one extraordinary fact: those men who pretend to take a vast interest in certain of the higher morals seem never able to exercise the simplest, the most necessary, and, in my opinion, the one essential virtue—politeness. All the more reason, therefore, to thank God that we have com- paratively few people obsessed with this notion of higher morals. I say "notion," because as a matter of fact I have never come across it, and therefore have no reason to believe in the actual existence of such a thing.

LADY. There is nothing new in that. As to polite-ness, there is some truth in what you say. Now before we approach the main subject of our discus-sion, perhaps you will attempt a proof that polite-ness is the one essential virtue. A trial proof, let us say, on which you may test your powers just as musicians test their instruments in the orchestra before the overture.

POLITICIAN. When the orchestra is tuning up, we hear only single disconnected sounds. I fear my proof would inflict on us a similar monotony; for hardly anybody would urge the opposite opinion— at least, not before the Prince comes in. Of course, when he arrives it would not be polite at all to speak of politeness.

LADY. Obviously. But what are your arguments?

POLITICIAN. I think you will agree that it is quite possible to live an enjoyable life in a society in which there was not a single person chaste, or dis-interested, or unselfish. I, at any rate, could always live in such society without feeling in the least uncomfortable.

LADY. In Monte Carlo, for instance?

POLITICIAN. In Monte Carlo, or anywhere else. Nowhere is there any need for even a single exponent of the higher morals. Now, you try to live in company where you cannot find a single polite man.

GENERAL. I don't know what kind of company you are talking about, but in the Khiva campaign[4] or in the Turkish campaign we should have fared ill if we had had no other virtue save politeness.

POLITICIAN. You may just as well say that some-thing besides politeness is necessary for a traveller in Central Africa. I am speaking of a regular every-day life in a civilised human society. For this life no higher virtues and no Christianity, so called, are necessary. (*To Mr. Z.*) You shake your head?

MR. Z. I have just recollected a sad incident, of which I was informed the other day.

LADY. What is it?

---

[4] A play upon words in Russian; the word for "company" stands also for "campaign." (Translator.)

MR. Z. My friend N. died suddenly.

GENERAL. Is he the well-known novelist?

MR. Z. That's the man.

POLITICIAN. The notices about his death in the Press were rather obscure.

MR. Z. Obscure they were, indeed.

LADY. But what made you think of him just at this moment? Was he killed by somebody's im- politeness?

MR. Z. Not at all! He died through his own excessive politeness and through nothing else.

GENERAL. Once more, it seems, it is impossible for us to agree.

LADY. Tell us the story, please, if you can.

MR. Z. There is nothing to conceal about it. My friend believed that politeness, if not the only virtue, is at least the first inevitable stage of social morality. He regarded it his duty to carry out all its prescrip- tions in the strictest possible manner. For instance, amongst other things he held it to include the reading of all the letters he received, even though they were sent by strangers, and also of all the books and pamphlets sent him with demands for reviews. He scrupulously answered every letter and as scrupu- lously wrote all the reviews demanded by his corre- spondents. He complied with all the requests and responded to all appeals made to him. As a result he found himself busy all day long attending to other people's affairs, and for his own work had to be satisfied with the night time. More than this, he accepted every invitation and saw all the visitors who caught him at home. So long as my friend was young and could easily stand the effects of frequent friendly potations, this galley-slave existence he had created for himself owing to his politeness merely annoyed him, and did not lead to tragedy: wine brought joy to his heart and saved him from despair. When he felt he would hang himself rather than stand it any longer, he would fetch out a bottle, from which he *drew* [1] that which helped him *drag*[5] his chains more cheerfully. But he was by no means a robust man, and at

---

[5] A play upon words in Russian. (Translator.)

the age of forty-five had to give up drinking strong liquors. In his new state of sobriety he found his hard labour worse than hell itself, and now I am told that he has committed suicide.

LADY. Do you mean to say that this was the result solely of his politeness? It was simply that he was out of his senses.

MR. Z. I have no doubt that the poor fellow had lost his spiritual and mental balance. But the word "simply" I think is hardly applicable to his case.

GENERAL. I, too, have known similar cases of madness. They would drive us mad too if we cared to examine them carefully: there is precious little that is simple about them.

POLITICIAN. One thing is clear, however, and that is, politeness has nothing to do with the case. Just as the Spanish crown is not responsible for the mad- ness of Councillor Popristchin,[6] so the duty of politeness is not answerable for the madness of your friend.

MR. Z. I quite agree. I am by no means opposed to politeness, I merely object to making any kind of absolute rule.

POLITICIAN. Absolute rules, like everything else absolute, are only an invention of men who are lacking in common sense and the feeling of reality. There are no absolute rules for me. I recognise only *necessary* rules. For instance, I know perfectly well that if I disregard the rules of cleanliness the result will be unpleasant to myself and to everyone else. As I have no desire to experience any objectionable sensations myself or to make other people experience them, I invariably observe the rule of washing myself daily, of changing my linen, and so forth, not because this is recognised by others, or by myself, or because it is something sacred which it is a sin to disregard, but simply because any disregard of this rule would be *ipso facto* materially inconvenient. The same applies to politeness in general, which, properly speaking, includes cleanliness as a part of it. It is much more *convenient* to me, as to everybody else, to observe rather than to break the rules of politeness. So I follow them. It suited your friend's fancy to imagine that politeness required from

---

[6] The hero of Gogol's *The Diary of a Madman*. (Translator.)

him answers to all letters and requests without considering his personal comforts and advantage. That sort of thing is surely not politeness at all, but merely an absurd kind of self-denial.

MR. Z. An abnormally developed conscientious- ness gradually became with him a mania, which eventually brought him to his ruin.

LADY. But it is awful that a man should have died because of such a foolish idea. How is it that you could not bring him to his senses?

MR. Z. I tried my best and had a powerful ally in a pilgrim from Mount Athos. He, by the way, was half a madman himself, but he had a remarkable personality all the same. My friend esteemed him greatly and often asked his advice in spiritual matters. The pilgrim instantly perceived the root of all the trouble. I knew the man very well and I was sometimes present at their conversations. When my friend began telling him of his moral doubts and to ask whether he was right in this or wrong in that, Barsanophius would immediately interrupt him with: "What, you are distressed about your sins? Give it up, my dear fellow, it is nothing. Let me tell you this: sin five hundred and thirty-nine times a day if you like, but, for Heaven's sake don't repent. To sin first and then to repent? Why, anybody can do that. Sin, by all means—and often! But repent? Never! For, if sin be evil, then to remember evil means to be vindictive, and nobody approves of that. And the worst vindictiveness of all is to remember your own sins. It is far better that you should re- member the evil done to you by others—there would be some benefit in this, as you would be careful with such people in future. But as for your own sins— forget them utterly. It is by far the better way. There is only one mortal sin—despondency, because it gives birth to despair, and despair is not even a sin, it is the death of spirit itself. Now, what other sins are there? Drunkenness? But a clever man drinks only so much as he has room for. If he has no more room left, he leaves off drinking. Now, a fool will get drunk even with spring water. So you see the real cause lies not in the strength of wine, but in the weakness of man. Some people are abso- lutely scorched up with vodka, and not only in- ternally, but externally as well. They go black all over and little flashes of blue flame flicker all over them; I have seen this with my own eyes. Now, how can you speak of the presence of sin when all the time hell itself is visibly coming out from you? And as to transgressions of the seventh command- ment, let me tell you candidly that it is as difficult to censure them as it is impossible to praise them. But I can hardly recommend them! There is ecstatic pleasure in it—one cannot deny it—but at the end it brings despondency and shortens one's life. If you don't believe me, see what a learned German doctor writes." Here Barsanophius would take an old-fashioned book from a shelf and would begin turn- ing over the leaves. "The title alone is worth some- thing, my dear fellow," he would say. "*The Microbiotica,* by Gufeland! Look here, page 176." And he would slowly read passages in which the German author earnestly warns his readers against extravagant waste of the vital forces. "You see now? Why should then a clever man suffer any loss? While one is young and thoughtless all sorts of things are pictured by the imagination. But later on—no, it is too costly an amusement. And as for recalling the past and grieving over it and sighing 'Alas! why have I damned myself? I have lost my innocence and spotted the purity of my soul and body!' Well, this, I can assure you, is mere foolish- ness. It simply means that you deliver yourself right into the hands of the Devil for his eternal amuse- ment. It flatters him, naturally, that your soul cannot go forward and upward, but stays marking time in the same old filthy spot. But here is my advice to you: as soon as he starts disturbing you by this sort of repentance, you simply spit and rub it with your foot, saying, 'See now, all my grievous sins, here they are. Ah, what a lot they mean to me. What rot!' I can assure you he will leave you alone—I speak from experience. . . . Well, what other sins have you got? Are you thinking of trying stealing? And if you did steal—there is no very great harm in it: nowadays everybody steals. There- fore, you mustn't think anything of such a trifle at all. The one thing to beware of is despondency. Should the memory of your past sins torment you, so that you wonder whether you have done harm to anybody or anything, then go to a theatre, or perhaps join some jolly friends, or read something funny. If, however, you insist on my giving you a rule, here is, then, one: Be firm in your faith, not through fear of sins, but because it is a joyful thing for a clever man to live with God; without God a man is utterly wretched. Try to understand the word of God. If you read it carefully there is comfort and happiness in every verse. Say your prayers with real uplifting of your soul once or twice every day. You never by any chance forget to wash yourself? No? Well, a sincere prayer is better for a man's soul than any amount of soap is for his body. Fast for the health of the stomach and your other organs. Just now every doctor is prescribing this for people on the wrong side of forty. Don't worry about other people's business, and don't go in for organised charity, if you have your own occupation. But give alms to the poor you meet, and never stay to count the cost. Give without stint to churches and monas- teries. Do not reckon the amount; in Heaven's clearing-house they will count it all up themselves. And then, you will be healthy in body and soul, and as for those hypocrites who would poke their noses into everybody's soul, because they find their own so hollow—with these you must never even speak."

Such talks as these had a very good effect on my poor friend, but even they could not at the last raise him from the mire of despondency; besides, lately he seldom met Barsanophius.

POLITICIAN. Do you know that this pilgrim of yours says in his way practically what I have been saying?

LADY. So much the better. But what a wonderful moralist he is, indeed! "Sin, if you must, but above all never repent." It appeals to me mightily!

GENERAL. I suppose he did not talk like this to everyone? In dealing with a murderer or a scoundrel he must surely have adopted quite a different tone.

MR. Z. That should be obvious. But as soon as he observes a man overwhelmed with moral doubts he at once becomes a philosopher and even a fatalist. He once delighted a very clever and educated old lady. Though she was Russian by faith, she was educated abroad, and having heard a great deal about our Barsanophius, she looked to him as to *"un directeur de conscience"* He, however, did not let her talk much about the worries of her soul. "And why do you worry yourself about all this rubbish? Who wants to hear it? I am only a common peasant, and yet it bores me to death. How can you imagine, then, that God can take any interest in it? And what is the good of talking about it? You are too old and too weak to begin improve- ment now." She afterwards herself told me this conversation, laughing and weeping at the same time. True, she tried to argue with him, but he completely persuaded her by a story from the life of two ancient hermits—Barsanophius narrated it to me and N. very often. It is a very fine story, only it will perhaps take too long to tell it.

LADY. Tell us in brief.

MR. Z. Well, I will. Two hermits had gone out into the Nitrian desert to save their souls. Their caves were not far distant from each other, but they themselves never talked together, except that they occasionally sang psalms, so that each could hear the other. In this way they spent many years, and their fame began to spread in Egypt and the sur- rounding countries. It came to pass that one day the Devil managed to put into their minds, both at the same time, one and the same desire, and without saying a word to each other they collected their work, baskets and mats made of palm leaves and branches, and went off to Alexandria. They sold their work there, and then for three days and three nights they sought pleasure in the company of drunkards and libertines, after which they went back to their desert.

And one of them cried out in bitterness and agony of soul:

"I am lost eternally! Cursed am I! For no prayers and penance can atone for such madness, such abominations! All my years of fasting and prayer gone for nothing! I am ruined, body and soul! "

The other man, however, was walking by his side and singing psalms in a cheerful voice.

"Brother," said the repentant one, "have you gone mad?"

"Why do you ask that ? "

"But why aren't you afflicting yourself ? "

"What is it that I should feel afflicted about?"

"Listen to him! Have you forgotten Alex- andria?"

"Well, what about Alexandria? Glory to God who preserves that famous and pious city! "

" But we, what did we do in Alexandria?"

"You know well enough yourself; we sold our baskets, worshipped St. Mark, visited other churches, called on the pious governor of the city, conversed with the good prioress Leonilla, who is always kind to monks. . . ."

"But didn't we spend the night in a house of ill fame?"

"God save us! No! We spent the evening and night in the patriarch's court."

"Holy martyrs! He has lost his mind. . . . Where then did we treat ourselves to wine ? "

"We partook of wine and food at the patriarch's table on the occasion of the Presentation of the Blessed Virgin."

"Poor, miserable creature! And who was it whom we kissed, not to mention worse things ? "

"We were honoured with a holy kiss on departing by the Father of Fathers, the most blessed arch- bishop of the great city of Alexandria and the whole of Egypt, Libya and Pentapolis, and judge of the World, Cyrus-Timotheus, with all the fathers and brothers of his God-chosen clergy."

"Are you making a fool of me? Or is it that the Devil himself has entered your soul as punishment for the abominations of yesterday? They were wretched libertines, you blackguard, that you kissed! "

"Well, I don't know which of us the Devil has entered: whether he has entered me, who am rejoicing in the gifts of God and in the benevolence of the godly priests, and am praising my Maker, as should every other living thing—or whether he has entered you, who are now raving like a madman and calling the house of our blessed father and pastor a house of ill fame, all the time insulting him and his God-loved clergy by calling them libertines."

"Oh, heretic you are! You offspring of Arian! Accursed mouth of Apollinarius that you are! "

At this the hermit who had been bewailing his lapse from virtue fell upon his comrade and began beating him with all his might. When the outburst was over, they walked silently to their caves. All night long the repentant one was wearing himself out with grief, filling the desert with his groans and cries, tearing his hair, throwing himself on the ground and dashing his head against it, whilst the other was quietly and happily singing his psalms. Next morning the repentant hermit was struck by a sudden thought: "By my many years of self-denial I had been granted a special blessing of the Holy Spirit which had already begun to reveal itself in miracles and apparitions. Now, if *after this* I gave myself up to the abominations of the flesh, I must have committed a sin against the Holy Spirit, which, according to the word of God, is for all eternity unpardonable. I cast a pearl, pure as heaven, before the swine of my reason—those devils—and they have crushed it to powder. Now they will most certainly turn on me and tear me to pieces. If, however, I am irrevocably doomed, what can I do here in the desert?" And so he went to Alex- andria and gave himself up to a wanton life. It so happened that soon he badly wanted money, and, in company with other dissolute fellows like himself, he murdered and robbed a wealthy merchant. The crime was discovered; he was tried by the city court and sentenced to death. He died an un- repentant sinner.

At the same time his old friend, continuing his life of devotion, attained to the highest degree of saintliness, and became famous for his great miracles, so that by the virtue of his mere word, women who had had no children for many years gave birth to men-children. When finally the day of his death arrived, his decrepit and withered body suddenly became resplendent with the beauty of youth. A wondrous light surrounded it; from it proceeded the perfume of sweet spices. After his death a monastery was built up over his relics, and his name passed from the Alexandrian Church to the Byzan- tine, and so to the church calendars of Kiev and Moscow. "It proves that I am telling the truth," Barsanophius used to say, in conclusion, "when I say that there is only one sin which does harm, and that is despondency." You see, every other crime the pilgrims both committed, but only one met his doom—he who gave himself up to grief.

GENERAL. You see, even monks have to be cheerful; whereas nowadays some would like to see soldiers bemoan their sins.

MR. Z. After all, then, though we have departed from the question of politeness, we have again approached our main subject.

LADY. And just at the psychological moment.

For here comes the Prince at last. We have been talking, Prince, in your absence, about politeness.

PRINCE. Please pardon me; I could not get here earlier. A bundle of all sorts of papers from our people, and various parcels of books, have arrived. I'll show you them by and bye.

LADY. Very well. Later, too, I will tell you the legend of two monks with which we have been con- soling ourselves in your absence. At present our Secret Monte-Carlist holds the floor. Now let us hear from you what you have to say about war after our discussion of yesterday.

POLITICIAN. From the. discussion of yesterday I have retained in my memory Mr. Z.'s reference to Vladimir Monomach, and the war story told by the General. Let these be our starting points for further discussion of the question. It is impossible to argue against the fact that Vladimir Monomach acted well when he fought and overcame the Polovtziens, and that the General also acted well when he annihilated the bashi-bazouks.

LADY. Then you agree with them?

POLITICIAN. I agree with that which I have the honour of stating before you now, viz., that both Monomach and the General acted in the way in which, *in the given circumstances*, they should have acted. But what follows from this to help us in judging the circumstances themselves, or for the justification and immortalisation of war and mili- tarism?

PRINCE. This is just what I was about to say.

LADY. Then you agree with the Prince now, don't you?

POLITICIAN. If you will allow me to explain my view of the subject, you will see yourself with whom and with what I do agree. My view is only a logical conclusion drawn from actual life and the facts of history. How can one argue against the historical importance of war when it is the main, if not the only, instrument by which the State has been created and gradually consolidated? Show me a single State which was founded and made secure otherwise than by war.

LADY. What about the United States?

POLITICIAN. I thank you for an excellent example. I am, however, speaking of the creation of a *State*. The United States, as a European *colony*, was, of course, founded not by war but by exploration, just as all other colonies were. But the moment this colony wished to become a State, it had to earn its political independence by means of a long war.

PRINCE. From the fact that the State has been created by war, which is, I agree, indisputable, you seem to conclude that war is all-important. In my opinion, however, the only conclusion which can be drawn from this fact is the unimportance of the State—for those people, of course, who no longer believe in the worship of violence.

POLITICIAN. Why all at once the worship of violence? What would it be for? Just you try to establish a stable human community outside the compulsory forms of the State, or yourself reject in practice everything that takes its life from the State —then you will be able to speak legitimately of the unimportance of the State. But until you do so, the State, and everything for which you and I are in- debted to it, will remain a colossal fact, whilst your attacks against it remain but empty words. Now, I say again that the supreme historical importance of war, as the principal condition in the creation of a State, is beyond any doubt. But I ask you: Is it not right to regard this great task of creating States as already completed in its broad outlines? As to the details, these can be settled without having recourse to such a heroic instrument as war. In ancient times and during the Middle Ages, when the world of European culture was merely an island in the midst of an ocean of more or less barbarous tribes, the military system was necessitated by the very instinct of self-preservation. It was at that time necessary to be always ready to repel any hordes which suddenly swooped down from an un-suspected quarter to trample down the feeble growth of civilisation. At present it is only the non- European element which can be described as the islands, for European culture has become the ocean which is gradually washing these islands away. Our scientists, explorers, and missionaries have searched the whole earth without finding anything which is likely to menace seriously our civilised world. Savages are being successfully exterminated, or are dying out ; whilst militant barbarians, like the Turks and Japanese, are being civilised and losing their liking for warfare. In the meanwhile, the process of uniting all the European nations in the common bond of civilized life . . .

LADY (*in a whisper*). Monte Carlo. . . .

POLITICIAN. . . . In the common bond of civilised life has grown to such an extent that war amongst these nations would really be something in the nature of fratricide, which could not be excused on any grounds now that peaceful settlement of inter- national disputes has become possible. It would be as fantastic in our time to solve such disputes by war as it would be to travel from St. Petersburg to Marseilles in a sailing boat or in a coach driven by a "troika." I quite agree, of course, that " A lonely sail is looming white in the blue mist of the sea" or "See the troika flitting wild"[7] sounds vastly more poetic than the screeching of railway engines or cries of *"En voiture, messieurs!"* In the same way I am prepared to admit the aesthetic superiority of the "bristling steel of lances" and of "with swing- ing step in shining array the army is marching along" over the portfolios of diplomats and the cloth-covered tables of peaceful Congresses. But the serious attitude towards this vital question must, obviously, be entirely independent of the aesthetic appreciation of the beauty which belongs not to real war (this, I can assure you, has very little of the beautiful), but to its reflection in the imagina- tion of the poet and artist. Well, then, once it has been understood by everybody that war, however interesting for poetry and painters (these, of course, could be well satisfied with past wars), is useless now, for it is a costly and risky means of achieving ends which can be achieved at much less cost and in a more certain way by other methods, *it follows then that the military period of history is over.* I am speaking, of course, *en grand*. The immediate disarmament of nations

---

[7] Quotations from popular poems by Lermontov and Poushkin. (Translator.)

is out of the question. But I firmly believe that neither ourselves nor our sons will ever see a great war—a real European war— and that our grandsons will learn only of little wars —somewhere in Asia or Africa and of those from historical works.

Now, here is my answer with regard to Vladimir Monomach. When it became necessary to protect the future of the newly-born Russian State, first from the Polovtziens, then from the Tartars, and so on, war was a most necessary and important enterprise. The same, with certain limitations, may be applied to the period of Peter the Great, when it was necessary to ensure the future of Russia as a *European* Power. But after that its importance has been becoming ever more disputable, and at the present day, as I have already said, the military period of history is over in Russia, just as it is everywhere else. And what I have said about our country can be applied, of course, *mutatis mutandis*, to the other European countries. In every one of them war was, in days gone by, the main and inevit- able means of defending and strengthening the existence of the State and the nation, and has everywhere lost its *raison d'être* when once this object has been attained.

I may say, by way of parenthesis, that I am puzzled to find some modern philosophers dis- cussing the rational basis of war, independently of the time. Has war any rational basis? *C'est selon*. Yesterday it probably had everywhere a rational basis; to-day it has a rational basis only somewhere in Africa and Middle Asia, where there are still savages. To-morrow it will be justified nowhere. It is remarkable that with the loss of its rational basis war is, though slowly, losing its glamour. This can be seen even in a nation so backward in the mass as our own. Judge yourself: the other day the General triumphantly pointed out the fact that all our saints are either monks or soldiers. I ask you, however, to what historical period does all this military holiness or holy militarism actually belong? Is it not that very period in which war was *in reality* the most necessary, salutary, and, if you will, most holy enterprise. Our saint-warriors were all princes of the Kiev and Mongolian periods, but I fail to recollect any lieutenant-general amongst them. Now, what is the meaning of it all? You have two famous warriors, having exactly the same personal right to saintship, and it is granted to one and refused to the other. Why is it? Tell me, why is Alexander the Nevsky, who overthrew the Livonians and Swedes in the thirteenth century, a saint, whereas Alexander Suvorov, who overcame the Turks and the French in the eighteenth century, is not? You cannot reproach Suvorov with any- thing incompatible with holiness. He was sincerely pious, used to sing publicly in the church choir and read out the Bible from the lectern, led an irre- proachable life, was not even any woman's lover, whilst his eccentricities make no obstacle to, but rather supply, a further argument for his being canonised. The sole difference is that Alexander the Nevsky fought for the national and political future of his country, which, half battered down in the East, could scarcely survive another battering in the West. The intuitive sense of the people grasped the vital importance of the position, and gave the Prince the highest reward they could possibly bestow upon him by canonising him. Whereas the achievements of Suvorov, though greatly superior in the military sense, particularly his Hannibalian passage of the Alps, did not respond to any pressing need; he was not obliged to save Russia, and so, you see, he has for ever remained merely a military celebrity.

LADY. But the leaders of the Russian army in 1812, though they were saving Russia from Napo- leon, yet failed to get canonized either.

POLITICIAN. Oh, well, "saving Russia from Napoleon"—that is merely patriotic rhetoric. Napoleon wouldn't have swallowed us up, nor was he going to. The fact that we finally got the upper hand certainly revealed our power as a nation and a State, and helped to awaken our national consciousness. But I can never admit that the war of 1812 was caused by any pressing necessity. We could very well have come to terms with Napoleon. But, naturally enough, we could not oppose him without taking some risks, and though the risks proved lucky for us, and the war was brought to an end in a way that greatly flattered our national self-esteem, yet its subsequent effects could hardly be regarded as really useful. If I see two athletes suddenly without any conceivable reason falling upon each other and one worsting the other, both suffering no harm to their health, I would perhaps say of the victor, "He is a good sport!" but the need of just this particular form of sportsmanship and of no other would remain for me very obscure. The fame of 1812, the national virtues revealed at that time, remain with us, whatever the causes of the war may have been.

> "The sacred verity of 1812
> Was still alive in people's eyes."

This is very good for poetry: "the sacred verity!" But I turn to what came out of that verity, and I find on the one side archimandrite Photius, Magnitsky, Araktcheiev, and on the other side, the Decabrists' conspiracy, and, *en somme*, that thirty years' long *régime* of belated militarism, which eventually brought us to the *débâcle* of the Crimean War.

LADY. And what about Poushkin?

POLITICIAN. Poushkin? Why Poushkin?

LADY. I have recently read in the papers that the national poetry of Poushkin owed its inspiration to the military glories of 1812.

MR. Z. And not without some special participa- tion of artillery, as the poet's name indicates.[8]

POLITICIAN. Yes; perhaps that is really how it is. To continue my argument, however. As years roll on the uselessness of our wars becomes ever clearer and clearer. The Crimean War is regarded in Russia as very important, as it is generally believed that the liberation of serfs and all the other reforms of Alexander II. were due to its failure. Even sup- posing this was so, the beneficial effects of an *unsuccessful* war, and only because it was unsuc- cessful, cannot, of course, serve as an apology for war in general. If I, without any satisfactory reason, try jumping off the balcony and put my arm out of joint, and later on this dislocation prevents me from signing a ruinous promissory note, I shall be glad afterwards that it had happened like that; but I will not say that it is generally recommended to jump off a balcony and not to walk down by

---

[8] "Poushkin"—of the "poushka"—of the gun. (Translator.)

the stairs. You will agree that when the head is not hurt there is no need for hurting the arm in order to escape signing ruinous agreements; one and the same good sense will save a man both from foolish leaps from a balcony and from foolish signa- tures. I believe that even if there were no Crimean War the reforms of Alexander II. would most prob- ably have been carried out, and perhaps in a more secure and far-reaching way. But I am not going to prove this now; we must see that we do not depart from our subject. At any rate, political acts cannot be rated at their indirect and unforeseen conse- quences; and as to the Crimean War, that is, its com- mencement brought about by the advance of our army to the Danube in 1853, it had no reasonable justification. I cannot call sensible the policy which one day saves Turkey from the smashing defeat inflicted on Mehmet Ali by the Pasha of Egypt, thus hindering the division of the Moslem world round two centres, Stambul and Cairo, which, it seems, would not have done us much harm; and which next day tries to destroy this same redeemed and reinforced Turkey, with the risk of running against the whole of the European coalition. This is not policy, but a sort of Quixotism. The same name I will apply also—I hope the General will pardon me this—to our last Turkish war.

LADY. And the bashi-bazouks in Armenia?

Didn't you approve of the General for annihilating them?

POLITICIAN. Pardon me, I maintain that at the present time war has become *useless*, and the story told by the General the other day bears this out particularly well. I quite understand that anybody whose military duty made him an active participant in the war, and who happened to come across irre- gular Turkish troops inflicting terrible barbarities upon the peaceful population, I say that that man, that every man (*looking at the Prince*) free from preconceived "absolute principles," was obliged by sentiment and by duty alike to exterminate those bashi-bazouks without mercy, as the General did, and not to worry about their moral regeneration, as the Prince suggests. But, I ask, in the first place, who was the real cause of all this wretched business? And, in the second place, what has been achieved by the military intervention? To the first question I can answer in all honour only by pointing to that bad militant policy which irritated the Turks by inflaming the passions and supporting the preten- sions of the Christian populations. It was only when Bulgaria began to swarm with revolutionary com- mittees and the Turks became alarmed at possible interference on the part of the European Powers, which would have led the State to inevitable ruin, that the Turks began to slaughter the Bulgarians. The same thing also happened in Armenia. As to the second question, what has come out of it? The answer supplied by recent events is so striking that nobody can help noticing it. Judge yourself : in 1877 our General destroys a few thousands of bashi-bazouks and by this *probably* saves a few hun- dreds of Armenians. In 1895, in the very same place, very much the same bashi-bazouks slaughter not hundreds but thousands, perhaps even tens of thousands of the population. If various corre- spondents can be trusted (though I myself would not advise anyone to do so), the number of people massacred was nearly half a million. Of course, this is all a fairy tale. But there can be little doubt that these later Armenian massacres were carried out on a much larger scale than the old Bulgarian ones. There you have the beneficent results of our patriotic and philanthropic war.

GENERAL. Now, understand it who can! Now it is bad policy which is to be blamed, now it is the patriotic war. One might believe that Prince Gorchakov and M. Hirs were soldiers, or that Disraeli and Bismarck were Russian patriots and philanthropists.

POLITICIAN. Is my statement really not clear enough? I have in view the indisputable connec- tion, and not some abstract or ideal one, but the wholly real, pragmatic connection between the war of 1877, which was brought about by our bad policy, and the recent massacres of Christians in Armenia. You probably know, and if you don't you will profit by learning it, that after 1878 Turkey, who could see her future prospects in Europe from the terms of the St. Stephen's agreement, resolved at any rate to secure her position in Asia. First of all she secured an English guarantee at the Berlin Con- gress. She, however, rightly believed that England would help her if she helped herself, and com- menced to reinforce and establish her irregular armies in Armenia, more or less those very " devils" which the General had to deal with. This proved a very sound policy; only fifteen years passed after Disraeli had, in exchange for Cyprus, guaranteed Turkey her Asiatic dominions, when English policy, in view of changed circumstances, became anti- Turkish and Armeniophile, whilst English agitators appeared in Armenia as Slavophile agitators did earlier in Bulgaria. At that moment those familiar to the General as "devils" found themselves "the men of the hour," and with the most polished manners helped themselves to the largest portion of Christian meat which had ever reached their teeth.

GENERAL. It is disgusting to listen to! And why should the war be blamed for this? Good Heavens! if only the wise statesmen had finished their business in 1877 as well as the soldiers did theirs, you may be sure there would have been not even a mention of any reinforcement or establishment of irregular armies in Armenia. Consequently, there would have been no massacres.

POLITICIAN. In other words, you mean to say that the Turkish Empire ought to have been totally destroyed?

GENERAL. Emphatically I do. I am sincerely fond of the Turks, and have much esteem for them. They are a fine people, especially when compared with all these nondescript Ethiopians. Yet I verily believe that it is well-nigh time for us to put an end to this Turkish Empire.

POLITICIAN. I should have nothing to say against this, if those Ethiopians of yours would be able to establish in its place some sort of Ethiopian Empire of their own. But up to the present they can only fight each other, and a Turkish Government is as much necessary for them as the presence of Turkish troops is necessary in Jerusalem for preserving the peace and well-being of the various Christian denominations there.

LADY. Indeed! I have always suspected that you would not object to handing over the Sepulchre to the Turks for ever.

POLITICIAN. And you, of course, think that this would be owing to my atheism or indifference, don't you? As a matter of fact, however, my wish to see the Turks in Jerusalem is the reflection of a faint but inextinguishable spark of religious sentiment which I still preserve from my childhood. I know positively that the moment the Turkish soldiers are withdrawn from the streets of Jerusalem all the Christians in the city will massacre each other, after having destroyed all the Christian shrines. If you doubt my impressions and conclusions, just ask any pilgrims whom you may trust, or, what is even better, go and see for yourself.

LADY. That I should go to Jerusalem? Oh, no! What could I see there? . . . No ; I should think twice before I did that!

POLITICIAN. Well, that only bears out my state- ment.

LADY. I cannot understand this at all. You argue with the General, and yet you both extol the Turks.

POLITICIAN. The General values them apparently as brave soldiers, and I do so as the guardians of peace and order in the East.

LADY. Fine peace and order, indeed, when some tens of thousands of people are suddenly and mercilessly slaughtered. Personally, I would prefer disorder.

POLITICIAN. As I have already had the honour of stating, the massacres were caused by the revolu- tionary agitation. Why should you then demand from the Turks a higher degree of Christian meek- ness and forbearance than is ever demanded from any other nation, not excepting a Christian one? Can you quote me a country where an insurrection has ever been quelled without recourse to harsh and cruel measures? In the case before us, in the first place the instigators of the massacres were not the Turks. In the second place, Turks proper took hardly any part in them, acting in most cases through the General's "evils." And in the third place, I am prepared to admit that the Turkish Government, by letting loose these "devils," over- did the thing; as Ivan IV. overdid it when he drowned ten thousand peaceful inhabitants of Novgorod; or as the commissioners of the French Convention overdid it by their *noiades* and *fusil- lades*; or lastly, as the English overdid it in India when they quelled the Mutiny of 1857. And yet there can be little doubt that should these various Ethiopians be left alone, there would be much more massacre than under the Turks.

GENERAL. Who told you I want to put these Ethiopians in the place of Turkey? Surely, the thing is very simple: we should take

Constanti- nople, we should take Jerusalem, and in the place of the Turkish Empire should form a few Russian military provinces, like Samarkand or Askhabad. As to the Turks, they, after they had laid down their arms, should in every way be satisfied and pleased, in religion as much as in everything else.

POLITICIAN. I hope you are not serious now, or I shall be obliged to doubt . . . your patriotism. Don't you see that if we started a war with such radical ends in view, this would certainly bring to life once more a European coalition against us, which our Ethiopians, liberated or promised libera- tion, would ultimately join. These latter under- stand very well that under the Russian power they would not be so free to express their national spirit.

And the end of it all would be that, instead of destroying the Turkish Empire, we should have a repetition—only on a grander scale—of the Sebas- topol *débâcle*. No, though we have indulged in bad politics sufficiently often, I am sure that we shall never see such madness as a new war with Turkey. If we do see it, then every Russian patriot must exclaim with despair: *Quem deus vult perdere, prius dementat*.

LADY. What does that mean?

POLITICIAN. It means: Him whom God would destroy, He first makes mad.

LADY. I am glad history is not made according to your argument. You are, I suppose, as much in favour of Austria as of Turkey, aren't you?

POLITICIAN. I need not enlarge upon this, as people more competent than myself the national leaders of Bohemia, for example have declared long ago: "If there were no Austria, Austria should be invented." The recent affrays in the Vienna Parliament supply the best possible illus- tration of this maxim, and are a vision in miniature of what must happen in these countries should the Hapsburg Empire be destroyed.

LADY. And what is your opinion about the Franco-Russian Alliance? You seem always to reserve it somehow.

POLITICIAN. Neither do I propose to go into the details of this delicate question just now. Speak- ing generally, I can say that *rapprochement* with such a progressive and rich nation as France is, at any rate, beneficial to us. On the other hand, this alliance is, of course, an alliance of peace and pre- caution. This is, at any rate, the meaning which is put on it in the high circles where it was concluded and is still supported.

MR. Z. As to the benefits of *rapprochement* between two nations for the development of their morals and culture, this is a complicated matter, which to me seems very obscure. But looking at it from the political point of view, don't you think that by joining one of the two hostile camps on the European continent we lose the advantages of our free position as neutral judge or arbiter between them; we lose our impartiality? By joining one side, and thereby balancing the powers of both groups, don't we create the possibility of an armed conflict between them? It is, for instance, clear that France alone could not fight against the Triple Alliance, whereas with the help of Russia she could certainly do so.

POLITICIAN. Your considerations would be quite correct if anybody had any wish to begin a European war. But I can assure you that nobody has such a wish. At any rate, it is much easier for Russia to prevent France from leaving the path of peace than it is for France to lure Russia to the path of war, undesirable, as a matter of fact, to both of them. The most reassuring thing, however, is the fact that not only are modern nations averse to waging war, but, what is more important, they *begin to forget how to do it*. Take, for example, the latest con- flict, the Spanish-American war. Well, was this a war? Now, I ask you: was it really a war? Mere dolls' play it was; an affray between a street brawler and a constable! "After a long and furious fight the enemy retreated, having lost two killed and one wounded. We sustained no losses." Or: "The whole of the enemy's squadron, after a desperate struggle with our cruiser *Money Enough,* surrendered at discretion. No losses either of killed or wounded were sustained on either side." And there you have the whole war. I am surprised that all seem to be so little surprised at this new char- acter of war—its bloodlessness, so to speak.

The metamorphosis has been taking place before our very eyes, as we all can remember the sort of bulletins published in 1870 and in 1877.

GENERAL. Wait a little with your surprise until two really military nations come into collision. You will see then what sort of bulletins will be issued!

POLITICIAN. I am not so sure. How long is it since Spain was a first-class military nation? Thank God, the past cannot return. It appears to me that just as in the body useless organs become atrophied, so it is in mankind: the fighting qualities have lost their usefulness, and so they disappear. Should they suddenly reappear again, I should be as much startled as if a bat suddenly acquired eagle eyes, or if men again found themselves with tails.

LADY. But how is it, then, that you yourself praised the Turkish soldiers?

POLITICIAN. I praised them as guardians of peace within the State. In this sense the military power or, as it is said, "the mailed fist," *manus militaris*, will yet for a long time be necessary for mankind. But this does not interfere with the fact that mili- tancy in the sense of disposition and ability to wage international wars, this national *pugnacity*, so to speak, must entirely disappear and is already disappearing before our eyes, degenerating into that bloodless, though not altogether harmless, form which is exemplified in Parliamentary squabbles. As, on the other side, the disposition to such dis- plays will apparently remain as long as there are conflicting parties and opinions, so in order to check them the *manus militaris* will necessarily remain in the State, even at the time when external wars, that is, wars between nations or States, will have long become merely things of the historical past.

GENERAL. That is to say, you liken the police to the coccyx, which still exists in man, although only the Kiev witches are credited with proper tails! How very witty! But aren't you just a little too ready with your comparison? Your conclusion is that just because some nation or other degenerates, becomes flabby, and can no longer fight, therefore the military virtues are decadent or lost all the world over! It is possible that under the introduction of "legislative measures" and "systems" even the Russian soldier may soften to jelly! Heaven preserve us!

LADY (*to the Politician*). You have not explained yet in what manner, war being excepted, such questions as, for instance, the Eastern Question should be solved. However wicked the Christian nations in the East may be, they do feel a desire to be independent at any cost, and the Turks do for this reason slaughter them. Surely you don't suggest that we should look on with folded arms? Supposing that your criticisms of the past wars are really sound, I shall ask, like the Prince, though in a different sense: "What are we to do now, should massacres begin somewhere again?"

POLITICIAN. But before they do begin, we must quietly exercise our judgment, and instead of a bad policy follow a good one, even though it be German; that is to say, we must not irritate the Turks, and must not shout when in our cups about raising the cross on the mosques. Instead of all this we must in a peaceful and friendly manner civilise Turkey for our mutual benefit: for ours, as much as her own. It depends entirely on us to make the Turks understand in the quickest time possible that slaughtering inhabitants in one's country is not only a bad thing in itself, but, what is the main point, that it has no use and yields no profit.

MR. Z. These suggestions of yours involve railway concessions and all sorts of trade and commercial interests, in which the Germans, I am sure, will forestall us, and competition with them in this direction would be a hopeless task.[9]

POLITICIAN. But why should we compete? If somebody does hard work for me, I shall be only too glad and thankful. If, however, this makes me cross with him, so that I ask: "Why did he do it and not I?" I am acting in a fashion which would be unworthy of a respectable man. In the same way it would be unworthy of such a nation as Russia to

---

[9] These words, which were written by me in Oct., 1899, were fully borne out in a month's time by the announced German-Turkish convention concerning Asia Minor and the Baghdad railway. (Author.)

imitate the dog-in-the-manger, which lying on the hay neither eats nor lets others eat. If others, using their own means, can do more quickly and in a better way the good thing which we also desire, then so much the more profitable is it for us. I ask you : were not all our wars with Turkey during the nine- teenth century waged only for the sake of safeguarding the human rights of the Turkish Chris- tians ? Now, what if the Germans achieve the same object in a sure, though peaceful, way by *civilising* Turkey? It is clear that had they been as firmly established in Asia Minor in 1895 as the English are in Egypt, you may take my word for it we should not have to discuss Armenian massacres any longer.

LADY. But you have already suggested that it is necessary to make an end of Turkey. Only you are, for some unknown reason, anxious to see her eaten up by the Germans.

POLITICIAN. It is just because the German policy has no desire to swallow such indigestible articles that I called it wise. Its object is more subtle: it is to bring Turkey into the company of the civilised nations, to help the Turks in educating themselves and making themselves capable of undertaking a just and humane control over nations which, owing to their mutual savage hostility, are unable to direct their own affairs peacefully.

LADY. What fairy tales are these? Who will ever think it possible to surrender a Christian people to the Turks for eternal control? I like the Turks myself for many things, but still they are barbarians, and their last word will always be violence. A European culture will only make them worse.

POLITICIAN. Exactly the same could be said about Russia at the time of Peter the Great, and even at a much later period. We remember "Turkish bar- barities," but how long is it since in Russia, and in other countries as well, that "Turkish barbarities" became unknown? 'The poor unhappy Christians groaning under the Moslem yoke!" And what about those who groaned under the yoke of our wicked landlords—were they Christians or pagans? Or what about the soldiers who groaned under the punishment of the rod? However, the only just and reasonable answer to these groans of the Russian peasants was the abolition of serfdom and of the rod, and not the destruction of the Russian Empire.

Why, then, must the answer to the Bulgarian and Armenian groans be of necessity the destruction of the State in which these groans are heard, but also of States where they need not be heard either?

LADY. It is one thing when disgusting things take place within a Christian State which can be easily reformed, and another thing when a Christian people is being oppressed by a non-Christian one.

POLITICIAN. The impossibility of reforming Turkey is merely a rooted prejudice which the Germans are disproving before our eyes, just as they earlier helped to destroy the prejudice of the inborn savagery of the Russian people. As to your distinction between "Christians" and "non-Chris- tians," you will do well to remember that for the victims of barbarities this question is lacking in interest. If anybody strips off my skin, I shall surely not ask him: "What is your religion, sir?" Neither shall I be at all consoled if I find out that the people torturing me are not only extremely unpleasant and disturbing to me, but on the top of this, being Christians themselves, are exceedingly abhorrent to their own God, who sees His com- mands openly defied. Speaking objectively, it cannot be denied that the "Christianity" of Ivan the Terrible, or Saltykova, or Arakcheiev[10] is not in any sense an advantage, but rather so utterly base that it is impossible to meet with its like in other religions. Yesterday the General was describing the dastardly deeds of the savage Kurds, and amongst other things he mentioned their Devil-worship. It is certainly very wicked to roast babies or grown-up people over a slow fire—I am quite prepared to call such acts devilish. It is a well-known fact, however, that Ivan the Terrible was particularly fond of this very roasting of men on a slow fire. He would even keep the fire under- neath well poked! And yet he was not a savage or a devil-worshipper, but rather

---

[10] The Moscow landlady of the middle of the 18th century, Saltykova, and the favourite of Alexander I., General Arakcheiev, have become famous in Russia for the monstrous atrocity with which they treated those under their power. (Translator.)

a man of keen intel- lect, and, for the age in which he lived, a man of wide learning, whilst at the same time he was also a theologist firmly attached to orthodoxy. But we need not probe so far into the remote past. Take the Bulgarian Stamboulov and the Servian Milan— are they Turks, or are they representatives of the so-called Christian nations? What is, then, this " Christianity " of yours if not an empty title, which carries with it no guarantee for anything?

LADY. One would think it is the Prince expound- ing his faith. How strange!

POLITICIAN. When obvious truth is concerned I am willing to be at one not only with our esteemed Prince, but even with Balaam's ass!

MR. Z. But if my memory does not fail me, your Excellency has kindly agreed to take the leading part in to-day's discussion—not with the idea of arguing about Christianity or the animals of the Bible. I can hear ringing in my ears your soulful prayer: "Only as little religion as possible! For God's sake, as little religion as you can help!" Remembering this, may it please your Excellency to return to the subject of our discussion and to explain one little thing that is puzzling me. It is this. As you have rightly stated, our object must be not the destruction of the Turkish Empire, but the work of its civilisation. On the other hand, as you also admitted on quite reasonable grounds, the advancement of Turkey along the path of culture will be, and is now, much better carried on by the Germans than it could ever be by us. Now, if both these statements are correct, will you be good enough to tell me what in your opinion there is left for Russia as an object for a special and solely Russian policy in the Eastern question?

POLITICIAN. A special policy for Russia? Why, it is clear that no such policy can exist. As you understand it, the *special* Russian policy is obviously one which would be set up and pursued by Russia independently of and against the plans of all the other European nations. But I must tell you that, as a matter of fact, no such policy has ever been pursued. We have deviated sometimes to its track, as, for instance, in the 'fifties, and later on in the 'seventies; but those regrettable deviations, giving examples of what I may call *bad* policy, have instantly brought their own reward in the shape of reverses of greater or smaller significance. Generally speaking, it is in no way possible to regard Russian policy in the Eastern question as independent or isolated. Its object from the sixteenth century and almost to the end of the eighteenth century was to defend the civilised world from the threatened invasion of the Turks, working in co-operation with Poland and Austria. As in that defence we were obliged to act conjointly with the Poles, the Cesarians, and the Republic of Venice, though free from any formal alliances, it is evident that that policy was a common and not an independent one. In the nineteenth century, and much more so in the twentieth century, its co-operative character must remain the same as before, though naturally its objects and means have of necessity changed. The problem now is not to defend Europe from Turkish barbarism, but to make the Turks themselves more European. For the old object the means required were military; for that of the present day they must be peaceful. Both in the first case as well as in the second the object itself remains constant: as for- merly the European nations were bound in solidarity by the interests of military defence, so to-day they are bound in solidarity by the interests of spreading civilisation.

GENERAL. And yet the old military solidarity did not prevent Richelieu and Louis XIV. from entering into alliances with Turkey against the Hapsburgs.

POLITICIAN. Just the bad Bourbon policy, which along with their senseless home politics duly re- ceived its just reward from history.

LADY. You call this history ? It used to be called regicide, if I am not mistaken.

POLITICIAN *(to Lady}*. The words matter little. What remains is the fact that no political mistake passes off without retribution. Those inclined to look that way, may see in this something mystical. So far as I am concerned, I find as little of it in this case as I should find were I, in my present age and position, to start drinking champagne, glass after glass, as if I were a young man, instead of satisfying myself with a milk diet. I should un- doubtedly become ill, and were I too persistent in my ancient *regime*, I should at last die off, as the Bourbons did.

LADY. You cannot dispute that your policy of milk diet *a la tongue* becomes exceedingly tedious.

POLITICIAN (*offended*). If I had not been inter- rupted, I should have long ago exhausted my sub- ject, and given place to somebody more enter- taining.

LADY. Please do not take me seriously. I was merely joking. On the contrary, I think you have been very witty . . . for your age and position.

POLITICIAN. So I say that we are at one with the rest of Europe in the object of reforming Turkey on the lines of culture, and we have not at present, nor can we ever have, any special independent policy. It must, however, be admitted that on account of our comparative backwardness in social development, in industry and trade, the share of Russia in this common cause of civilising the Turkish Empire cannot at present be very great. The foremost importance which our country had as a military State cannot, of course, be retained by us now. Predominance is not acquired for nothing; it must be earned. We earned our military importance not by mere bluff, but by actual wars and victories. In the same way, our importance in the work of civilisation must be earned by actual labour and successes in peaceful callings. As the Turks had to fall back before our military victories, they will now retire before those who prove themselves to be strongest in the sphere of peaceful progress. What is there left for us to do, in that case? You will hardly meet anywhere now with that blatant insanity which believes that the mere ideal of the imaginary raising of the cross on St. Sophia is a more powerful force in itself than is the actual superiority of the Germans.

GENERAL. The only thing is that this cross must not be a mere ideal.

POLITICIAN. But who will materialise it for you? So long as you have not found the means to do so, the only thing demanded by our national ambition —within the reasonable limits, of course, in which this feeling could be recognised at all—is to double our efforts so that we could as quickly as possible come into line with other nations in what we lag behind them, and by doing so, gain the time and effort wasted on various Slav committees and similar poisonous nonsense. Besides, if we are as yet powerless in Turkey, we are already capable of playing a leading part in civilising Central Asia, and particularly the Far East, whither, it appears, the history of the world is transferring its centre of gravity. Owing to her geographical situation, and other advantageous conditions, Russia can do more there than any other nation, except, of course, England. It follows, then, that the object of our policy in this respect must be to secure a permanent and amiable understanding with England, so that our co-operation with her in the work of civilisation may never change into a senseless hostility and unworthy competition.

MR. Z. Unfortunately, some such transformation always comes about—with single individuals as much as with nations, as if it were a part of their destiny.

POLITICIAN. It is true, they do happen. On the other hand, I don't know of a single case in the life of men, or in the life of nations, when hostility and envy displayed towards their coadjutors in a common cause have ever helped to make any one of them stronger, richer, and happier. This universal experience, to which not a single exception could be found, is being made use of by clever people. And I believe that such a clever nation as Russia will not fail to make use of it either. To quarrel with the English in the Far East—why, this would be the most utter madness, not to speak of the in- decency of indulging in domestic quarrels before strangers. Or do you perhaps think that we are more closely related to the yellow-faced Chinese than to the compatriots of Shakespeare and Byron ?

MR. Z. It is a delicate question.

POLITICIAN. Then we'll leave it alone for a time. Here you have something else to consider. From what I have said before, you already know that I recognise only two objects for the Russian policy: firstly, the maintenance of peace in Europe (for every European war at the present stage of historical evolution would amount to an insane and criminal internecine struggle); and secondly, the civilisation of the barbarian nations which are within the sphere of our influence. Now, if you accept my point of view you will see that both these objects, apart from their intrinsic value, are strikingly connected with each other, serving to further the realisation of each other, and that they are mutually interdepen- dent for their very existence. It is obvious, indeed, that if we really do all we can to give the benefits of civilisation to the barbaric countries, in which work all Europe is equally interested, we draw to- gether the bonds of solidarity between ourselves and other nations; whilst consolidating European unity we, by this very fact, strengthen our influence among barbarous nations, as we thus leave them no hope of successful resistance. Don't you think that if the yellow man knew that all Europe were behind Russia, we could do in Asia anything we wish? If, however, he saw that Europe were not behind Russia, but against her, he would not hesitate even to attack our frontiers, and we should have to defend ourselves on two fronts, over a line ten thousand versts long. I do not believe in the " Yellow Peril," because I do not admit the possibility of a European war. But given the latter, we should, of course, have to fear even the Mongolians.

GENERAL. To you a European war or a Mon- golian invasion seems to be absolutely out of the range of possibility. But I must confess I have very little faith in your "consolidarity of the European nations " and the coming " peace of the world." Somehow it seems to be highly unnatural, and ex- ceedingly unlikely. In the old Christmas hymn you hear sung: "Peace on earth and goodwill towards men." This means that peace will reign on the earth only when goodwill is established among men. But where is this goodwill now? Have you ever seen it? To be quite frank, both you and I feel a real and sincere goodwill only to one European power—the principality of Monaco. Inviolable, also, is our peace with it. To regard, however, the Germans or the English as members of our own family, to feel that their benefit is our benefit, their pleasure is our pleasure—such a "consolidarity," as you call it, with the European nations, I am sure, we shall never have.

POLITICIAN. Why "we shall never have," when it is already with us, when it is in the very nature of things? We are at one with the European Powers for the simple reason that we are Europeans our- selves. This has been an accomplished fact since the eighteenth century, and neither the total lack of culture amongst the Russian masses, nor the unfor- tunate chimeras of the Slavophiles, will ever be able to alter it.

GENERAL. Well, but do the Europeans agree among themselves? The French with the Germans, for instance; the English with both of these? It is rumoured that even the Swedes and the Nor- wegians have somewhere lost their consolidarity !

POLITICIAN. What a forceful argument! But what a pity it is that all its force rests on a defective basis on the total neglect of historical fact. I will ask you a question : " Would Moscow have been at one with Novgorod at the time of Ivan III., or Ivan the Terrible?" Will you on the strength of this deny the consolidarity of the Moscow and Novgorod provinces in the common interests of the State?

GENERAL. Oh, no; not at all. But this I will say: let us wait a little before declaring ourselves Euro- peans—at least until that historic moment when all the European nations are as firmly bound together as our provinces are in the Russian State. You will surely not advise us to tear ourselves to pieces in working for our consolidarity with all other Euro- peans, when they themselves are at daggers drawn ?

POLITICIAN. You will have it "at daggers drawn"! But you need not worry. Not only will you be saved from the necessity of tearing yourself to pieces between Norway and Sweden, but from doing so between France and Germany, and for the simple reason that they will never come to a rupture. At present it seems to be evident. Only in Russia can you find a good many people still taking for France that insignificant group of adventurers who should be, and must be, put in prison: let them *there* display their nationalism and preach a war with Germany.

LADY. It would really be a very good thing if it were only possible to put in prison all those who foment strife among the nations. But I think you are wrong.

POLITICIAN. Of course, what I have said must be taken *cum grano sails*. It is quite true that on the surface Europe has not yet become consolidated into one whole. But I still stand by my historical analogy. For instance, in our country in the sixteenth century, separation among various pro- vinces, though still present, was at its last gasp, whilst the unity of the State had long ago ceased to be a dream and was actually shaping itself into definite forms. So in a similar way in modern Europe, though national antagonism is still existent, particularly amongst the ignorant masses and half-educated politicians, it is not strong enough to transform itself into any considerable action : that it will not go so far as to lead to a European war I am positively certain. As to the goodwill of which you are speaking, General, to tell you the truth I fail to see it, not only amongst different nations, but within any nation itself, or even within single families. If you do meet it occasionally, it does not go farther than the first generation. Well then, what conclusion can be drawn from this ? Certainly not that this supplies the reason for intestine wars and fratricide. Similarly, in international relation- ships. The French and Germans may dislike each other if they wish, but let them abstain from actual fighting. I am sure that there won't be any.

MR. Z. This is very probable. But even regard- ing Europe as one whole, we cannot conclude from this that we ourselves are Europeans. You know there is an opinion, which has become fairly popular during the last twenty years, that Europe, that is, the combination of all the German-Latin nations, is really a distinct type characterised by political unanimity and by common culture and history; it is further maintained that we, Russians, do not belong to this group, but constitute a separate Greco- Slavonic type.

POLITICIAN. I have heard of this variety of Slavo- philism, and even have had occasion to speak with some of those holding this view. Now, there is one thing I have noticed about this theory, and it seems to me to give a decisive answer to the whole problem. It is a curious thing that all these gentle- men who argue in glowing perorations against Europe, and our being Europeans, can never be satisfied with the assumption of our Greco-Slavonic origin, but must always plunge headlong into a belief in some sort of Chinaism, Buddhism, Tibet- ism, and other Indo-Mongolian Asiaticisms. Their alienation from Europe is directly proportional to their gravitation to Asia. Now, what does it all mean? Let us admit that they are right in their view of Europe, that she is spiritually wrong. Why, however, this fatal running to the other extreme, to this aforesaid Asiaticism? Ah! And whither has the Greco-Slavonic nucleus vanished? No! tell me, where has it gone? Ah? And yet it is in that very nucleus that one would expect to find the very sub- stance of the thing! Ah? There you are, you see. You may drive nature out through the door, but she will get back through the window. And nature in this case is the fact that no independent Greco- Slavonic type of historic culture exists at all; but there has been, is, and always will be, Russia as the great borderland of Europe towards Asia. Such being the actual position of our country, it is only too natural that it feels the influence of the Asiatic element to a much greater extent than the rest of Europe, and this is all that makes up our imaginary originality. Byzantium herself was original, not through anything of her own, but only because of an admixture of the Asiatic element. Whilst with us, from time immemorial, and particularly since the days of the Mongolian yoke, this element has be- come a part of our nature, our second soul, so to speak, so that the Germans could say about us, sighing as they did so:

"Zwei Seelen wohnen, ach! in *ihrer* Brust
Die eine will sich von der andern trennen."

It is impossible for us to get rid of this second soul, nor is it desirable; for we owe a great deal to it. In order, however, that we may save ourselves from being torn to pieces in such a conflict, as is suggested by the General, it has been necessary that one soul should establish a decisive supremacy over the other, and it stands to reason that this soul should be the better of the two—that it should develop an intellect which is really the more power- ful, the more capable of further progress, and the more highly endowed with spiritual possibilities. Such supremacy was actually established at the time of Peter the Great. But the ineradicable (though finally overpowered) affinity of our soul with Asia even after that led certain minds into meaningless dreams that some chimerical revision of the his- torical question would settle it once and for ever.

Hence Slavophilism, the theory of an original type of historical culture and all the rest of it. As a matter of fact, we are *irrevocably Europeans*, but with an Asiatic sediment at the bottom of our soul. To me it is clear even grammatically. What is

"Russian " in the grammatical sense ? An adjec- tive. But what is the noun to which it refers?

LADY. I think the noun is " man," the Russian man.

POLITICIAN. No, that is too general and indefinite. Red Indians and Eskimos are also men, but I can- not agree in regarding as my noun what is common to me and the Redskins and the Eskimos.

LADY. There are things, you know, which are common to all human beings: love, for instance.

POLITICIAN. Well, that is even more general, How can I regard love as my specific property when I know that all other animals, and even mis- creants, have it in their nature ?

MR. Z. The question is no doubt very com- plicated. I am, for example, a man of meek character, and in love would be more at one with a white or blue-grey dove than with the black Moor Othello, though he also is called a man.

GENERAL. At a certain age every sensible man is at one with the white doves.[11]

LADY. Whatever is this?

GENERAL. This pun is not for you, but only for us with his Excellency.

POLITICIAN. Leave it alone, please, do leave it alone. *Trêve de plaisanteries*. Surely we are not on the stage of the Michael Theatre. I wished to say that the correct noun for the adjective "Russian" is "European." We are *Russian Europeans*, as there are English, French, and German Euro- peans. If I feel myself a European, would it not be stupid of me to argue that I am some Slavo-Russ or Greco-Slav? I am as positively certain of being a European as I am of being a Russian. I

---

[11] "White Doves" is the name of a Russian religious sect accused of immoral tendencies. (Translator.)

can, and perhaps even must, pity and protect every man, as every animal too: "Happy is he who shows mercy even to animals"; but I shall regard myself at one, *of the same family*, not with Zulus or Chinamen, but only with the nations and men who have created and preserved all those treasures of culture which form my spiritual food, and which afford me my highest pleasures. Before everything else it was necessary that these chosen nations should form and consolidate themselves, and should resist the on- slaught of the lower elements. For this, war was necessary and war was a holy enterprise. At present they possess the necessary form and strength, and there is nothing they need fear, except internal strife. Now the time has arrived for peace and the peaceful expansion of European culture over all the world. All must become Europeans. The idea expressed by "European" must be as all-embracing as that expressed by "man," and the idea of the European civilised world identical with that of man- kind. In this lies the meaning of history. At first there were only Greek Europeans. They were fol- lowed by the Roman ones. Next there arose all kinds of others, first in the West, later in the East; then there came Russian Europeans; later—beyond the ocean—the American Europeans; and now must come Europeans who are Turkish, Persian, Indian, Japanese, and possibly even Chinese. The "Euro- pean " is a notion with definite contents and an ever- expanding capacity. Note here one important distinction: every man is just as much a man as any other. Therefore, if we take as our noun this abstract symbol, we are bound to come to the all- levelling equality, and the nation of Newton and Shakespeare will have to be valued no more highly than certain Redskins. This would be too absurd for words, and subversive of practice. But if my noun is not a man in general, not that empty space with two feet, but a man as a bearer of culture, that is, a European, then nothing is left to support this absurd universal equality. The idea of a European, or what is the same, the idea of culture, possesses a measure for defining the relative virtues or values of various races, nations, individuals. A sensible policy cannot but take into account all these varia- tions in value. If it does not do so, if it, for instance, places on the same level a comparatively civilised Austria and some half-wild tribes of Herzegovina, this sort of thing will at once lead us to those stupid and dangerous adventures for which our last pillars of Slavophilism are still longing. *Il y a européen et européen.* Even after the cherished and, I hope, not far-distant hour has struck, when Europe or the civilised world will really coincide in extent with the total population of the world, even then there will remain in the unified and pacified mankind all those natural and historically determined gradations and shades in the values of various cultures which will determine our relations with other nations. Even in the triumphant and all-embracing kingdom of the higher culture, just as much as in the kingdom of Heaven—one glory is of the sun, another glory of the moon, yet other glories of the stars, for one star differs from another in glory—this is, I believe, how it is said in the Catechism, isn't it? How much more is it necessary to guard ourselves from an all- levelling equality in days when this object, though near, is not yet realised? At the present time, for instance, the papers have told us of more dissensions between England and the Transvaal—that the Boers are even threatening England with a war.[12] I can already see how all sorts of journalists and politicians in Russia, and most probably all over the Continent, will take up arms against England and will cry themselves hoarse in defence of those poor and oppressed Boers. But it is the same as if our most esteemed, worthy, well-known and learned Mr. Martens, having entered a neighbouring shop to buy something, was suddenly subjected to a violent attack by a dirty shop-boy shouting: "The shop is mine; you are a stranger here; if you don't clear off I will stifle or kill you!"—what time he is already trying to stifle him. Of course, one would feel pity for our esteemed Mr. Martens who fell a victim to such a rascally trick. But if this actually happened, I should certainly feel some moral satisfaction if my esteemed friend, having properly thrashed the rascal, had sent him by way of the police court to a home for young criminals. Instead of this, how- ever, we see various respectable people encouraging him and spurring him on. "Clever boy! Fancy a little chap like that being plucky enough to tackle

---

[12] The discussion took place in April, 1898. (Author.)

such a great hulking fellow! Go for him, Tommy; we will back you up when you want it! " How dis- gusting this is! Why, these Boer keepers and breeders of cattle have not brains enough to pro- claim themselves Dutchmen, with whom they are bound by blood-ties. Holland is a real nation, highly cultured, and with great merits to her credit. But no! They regard themselves as a separate nation; they want to create a country of their own. The damned rascals!

LADY. In the first place, you need not swear. And in the second, tell me what this Transvaal is like, and what kind of people live in it.

MR. Z. The people living there are a mongrel breed of Europeans and negroes; they are neither white nor black; they are "bur'i" (boers)[13].

LADY. Again a *calembour*?

POLITICIAN. And a very high-grade one!

MR. Z. What are the *boers*, such are also the calem*bours*. Though if you don't care for this colour, they have there also an *Orange* republic.

POLITICIAN. Speaking seriously, these Boers are of course Europeans, but only bad ones. Separated from their great motherland, they have to a great extent lost their former culture. Surrounded by savages, they have become wilder and coarser them- selves. Now to place them on the same level as the English, and to go even so far as to wish them success in the struggle with England—*cela n'a pas de nom !*

LADY. Didn't your Europeans sympathise with the Caucasian mountaineers when they fought Russia in defence of their independence? And are not Russians far more civilised than Caucasians?

POLITICIAN. I would not care to enlarge upon the motives of this sympathy of Europe with the Caucasian tribesmen. The only thing I will say is that we must assimilate the general European spirit and not be influenced by the accidental stupidities of this or that brand of European. From the bottom of my heart I regret, of course, that England, in order to pacify these conceited barbarians, will apparently be compelled to use such an obsolete and historically condemned weapon as war. But if it proves inevitable owing to the degraded state of mind of these Zulus—I

---

[13] A play upon words. In Russian "bur'i" means both boers and brown. (Translator.)

mean to say these Boers, encouraged by the foolish envy of England nursed by the Continent, I shall naturally eagerly wish that the war may end as soon as possible with the complete defeat of these African ruffians, so that nobody ever hears talk of their independence again. Should they prove successful and owing to the distance of their country from England this is not altogether impossible—it would be a triumph of barbarism over culture, and to me as a Russian, that is, a European, the day when that happened would be a day of deep national mourning.

MR. Z. (*to the General, in a low voice*). Ah, how well statesmen can speak. Altogether like that Frenchman: "Ce sabre d'honneur est le plus beau jour de ma vie."

LADY. No; I can't agree with you. Why should not we sympathise with these transboers? We sympathise with William Tell, for instance, do we not?

POLITICIAN. Well, if only they had created their own poetical legend, had inspired such artists as Schiller and Rossini, and had produced from among themselves anybody equal to Jean Jacques Rousseau, or any other writers or scientists—then the thing would be quite different.

LADY. But all that kind of thing happens after- wards; at first the Swiss themselves were shepherds like the Boers. But take other nations. Were the Americans, when they rose against the English to win independence, in any way distinguished in cul- ture? It is true they were not "bur'i"; they were perhaps a little "red-skinned," and used to strip off each other's scalps—according to Captain Mayne Reid. And yet even Lafayette sympathised with them, and was right, because now, for instance, in Chicago they have managed not only to unite all the religious bodies, but they have made an exhibition of them into the bargain. Nobody has ever seen such a thing before. Paris also wanted to gather together all its religions for the coming exhibition, but nothing came of it, as you doubtless know. One abbe, Victor Charbonnell, strove particularly hard for this union of religion. He wrote a few letters even to me—he was so nice. Only all the religions refused to join. Even the Great Rabbi declared: "For religion we have the Bible, and an exhibition has nothing to do with it." Poor Charbonnell was in such despair that he renounced Christ and pub-lished in the papers that he had retired from the service of religion and had a profound respect for Renan. He ended also very badly. According to somebody who wrote to me, he either got married or took to drink. Then our Nepliuev also tried, and he was disappointed in all religions. He wrote to me once—he was such an idealist—to the effect that he relied only on a united mankind. But how can you show a united mankind at a Paris exhibition? I think this merely a fancy. However, the Ameri-cans managed their business very well indeed. Each creed sent them a clergyman. A Catholic bishop was made chairman. He read them the "Pater noster" in English, and the Buddhist and Chinese priest idol-worshippers replied to him with all courtesy: "Oh, yes! All right, sir! We do not wish evil to anybody, and ask only for one thing: keep your missionaries as far from our coun-tries as you possibly can. Because your religion is exceedingly good for you, and if you do not observe it, it is not our fault; whilst our religion is the best for us." And it finished so well that there was not even a single fight! Everybody wondered. Now you see how good the Americans have become! Perhaps the modern Africans will in time be like these same Americans. Who knows?

POLITICIAN. Everything is possible, of course. Even the veriest gutter-snipe may later become a scientist. But before this happens you should for his own benefit give him more than one good hiding.

LADY. What language! *Decidement vous vous encanaillez.* And this is all from Monte Carlo! *Qui est-ce que vous fréquentez* là *has? Les families des croupiers sans doute.* Well, that concerns no-body but yourself. I would only ask you to prune your political wisdom a little bit, as you keep us from our dinner. It is time we finished.

POLITICIAN. I really wanted to sum up what I have said—to put head and tail together.

LADY. I have no faith in you. You will never finish of your own accord. Let me help you to ex-plain your thought. You wanted to say, didn't you, that times have changed; that before there were God and war, but now, instead of God, culture and peace. Isn't it so?

POLITICIAN. Well, I think it is near enough.

LADY. Good! Now what God is I do not know, nor can I explain. But I feel it all the same. As to your culture, I have not even a feeling for it. Will you then explain to me in a few words what it is?

POLITICIAN. What are the elements of culture, what it embraces—you know yourself: it includes all the treasures of human thought and genius which have been created by the chosen spirits of the chosen nations.

LADY. But these "chosen spirits" and their crea- tions differ alarmingly. You have, for instance, Voltaire and Rousseau and Madonna, and Nana, and Alfred De Musset and Bishop Philaret. How can you throw all these into one heap and set up this heap for yourself in place of God?

POLITICIAN. I was also going to say that we need not worry ourselves about culture as an historical treasury. It has been created, it is existing, and let us thank God for the fact. We may, perhaps, hope that there will be other Shakespeares and Newtons, but this problem is not within our power and pre- sents no practical interest. There is, however, an- other side to culture, a practical one, or if you like a moral one, and this is what in private life we call politeness, civility. To the superficial eye it may appear unimportant, but it has an enormous and singular significance for the simple reason that it is the only quality which can be universal and obligatory: it is impossible to demand from anybody either the highest virtue, or the highest intellect or genius. But it is possible and necessary to demand from everybody politeness. It is that *minimum* of reasonableness and morality which allows men to live like true human beings. Of course, politeness is not *all* culture, but it is a necessary *condition* of every form of cultured conduct, just as knowledge of reading and writing, though not the sum total of education, is a necessary condition to it. Politeness is cultured conduct, à l*usage de tout le monde*. And we are actually able to see how it spreads from private relationships amongst people of the same class to social relationships amongst different classes, and so to political or international relation- ships. Some of us can surely still remember how in our youth people of our class were allowed to treat the lower classes without any civility at all. Whereas at present a necessary and even compul- sory politeness has overstepped this class boundary, and is now on the way to overstep international boundaries as well.

LADY. Do, please, speak briefly. I see what you are driving at. It is that peaceful politics amongst the States is the same as politeness amongst indi- viduals, isn't it?

POLITICIAN. You are quite correct. It is evi- denced in the very words "politeness" and "politics," which obviously are closely related to each other. A remarkable thing is that no special feelings are necessary for this, no such *goodwill,* as was to no purpose mentioned by the General. If I do not fall upon anybody and do not furiously bite his head, this does not mean that I have any good- will towards that person. On the contrary, I may nurse in my soul the most rancorous feelings, but as a cultured man I cannot but feel repulsion at biting anybody, and, what is more important, I understand full well that the result of it will be anything but savoury, whilst if I abstain from it and treat this man in a polite manner, I shall lose nothing and gain much. Similarly, whatever may be the antipathies existing between two nations, if they have reached a certain level of culture they will never come to *voies de fait,* that is, to war, and for the patent reason that, in the first place, the real war—not that portrayed in poetry and pictures, but as actually experienced—with all those corpses, foul wounds, crowds of rough and filthy men, the stoppage of the normal order of life, destruction of useful buildings and institutions, of bridges, rail- ways, telegraphs—that a thing so horrid as this must be positively repulsive to a civilised nation, just as it is repulsive to us to see knocked-out eyes, broken jaws, and bitten-off noses. In the second place, at a certain stage of development, the nation under- stands how profitable it is to be civil to other nations and how damaging to its own interests it will be if it fights them. Here you, of course, have a number of gradations: the fist is more cultured than the teeth, the stick is more cultured than the fist, and the symbolical slap in the face is even more cultured still. Similarly, wars also can be conducted in a more or less savage way; the European wars of the nineteenth century more resemble a formal duel between two respectable persons than a fight be- tween two drunken labourers. But even this is only a transitional stage. Note that even the duel is out of fashion in advanced countries. Whereas back- ward Russia mourns her two greatest poets who have fallen in a duel; in more civilised France the duel has long ago changed into a bloodless offering to a bad and effete tradition. *"Quand on est mort c'est qu'on n'est plus en vie"* M. De-la-Palliss would say, and I am sure we shall still see with you how duels together with war will be relegated for ever to the archives of history. A compromise cannot last long here. Real culture requires that every kind of *fighting* between men and nations should be, entirely abolished. Anyhow, peaceful politics are the measure and the outward sign of the progress of culture. This is why, however anxious I am to please the worthy General, I still stand by my state- ment that the literary agitation against war is a welcome and satisfying fact. This agitation not only precedes, but actually expedites the final solution of a problem long since ripened. With all its peculiarities and exaggerations, this campaign acquires importance by its emphasising in the public consciousness the main line of historical progress

A peaceful, that is, civil, i.e., universally profitable settlement of all international relations and con- flicts—such is the fundamental principle of sound politics for civilised mankind. Ah? (*to Mr. Z.*) You want to say something?

MR. Z. Oh, it's nothing. It is only about your recent remark that peaceful politics is the symptom of progress. It reminds me that in Tourguenev's *Smoke* some person, speaking just as reasonably, says "Progress is a symptom." Don't you think, then, that peaceful politics becomes a symptom of a symptom?

POLITICIAN. Well, what of it? Of course, every- thing is relative. But what is your idea after all?

MR. Z. My idea is that if peaceful politics is merely a shadow of a shadow, is it worth while to discuss it so long? Itself and all that shadowy pro- gress? Wouldn't it be much better to say frankly to mankind what

Father Barsanophius said to the pious old lady: "You are old, you are feeble, and you will never be any better."

LADY. Well, it's now too late to talk about this. (*To the Politician.*) But you see what a practical joke this politico-politeness of yours has played on you.

POLITICIAN. What is that?

LADY. Simply that your visit to Monte Carlo, or *par euphemisme*, to Nice will have to be put off to-morrow!

POLITICIAN. Why will it?

LADY. Because these gentlemen here want to reply to you. And as you have been speaking with such prolixity as to leave no time for their replies, they are entitled to do so to-morrow. And surely, at a time when a company of cultured people is busy refuting your arguments, you would scarcely permit yourself to indulge in more or less forbidden pleasures in the company of uneducated croupiers and their families? This would be a *comble* of impoliteness. And what would be left then of your "obligatory minimum of morality"?

POLITICIAN. If that is the case, I must put off for one day my visit to Nice. I am interested myself to hear what can be said against my axioms.

LADY. That's splendid! Now I think everybody is really very hungry, and but for the culture you preach would have long ago made a dash for the dining-room.

POLITICIAN. *Il me semble du reste que la culture et l'art culinaire se marient très bien ensemble.*

LADY. Oh, oh! I must not listen to stuff like this!

(*Here all the rest, exchanging feeble witticisms, hastily followed the lady of the house to the dinner awaiting them.*)

THIRD DISCUSSION

Audiatur et tertia *pars*

THE THIRD DISCUSSION.

Audiatur et **tertia** *pars*

THIS time, in accordance with the general wish, we met in the garden earlier than usual, so that we might have leisure to finish the discussion. Some- how all were in a more serious mood than yesterday.

POLITICIAN (*to Mr. Z.*). I believe you wanted to make some statement about what I said last after- noon, did you not?

MR. Z. Yes. It has to do with your definition that peaceful politics is a symptom of progress. It brought to my mind the words of a character in Tourguenev's *Smoke*, that "progress is a symp- tom." I don't know what that character meant exactly, but the literal meaning of these words is perfectly true. Progress is certainly a symptom.

POLITICIAN. A symptom of what?

MR. Z. "It is a pleasure to talk with clever people."[14] That is just the question to which I have been leading. I believe that progress—a visible and accelerated progress—is always a *symptom of the end*.

POLITICIAN. I can understand that if we take, for instance, creeping paralysis. Its progress is a symptom of the end. But why should

---

[14] A Russian proverb. (Translator.)

the, progress of culture and cultured life always be a symptom of the end?

MR. Z. It is not so obvious, no doubt, as in the case of paralysis, but it is so all the same.

POLITICIAN. That you are certain of it is quite clear, but it is not clear to me at all what it is you are so certain of. And, to begin with, encouraged by your praise, I will again put you that simple question of mine which seemed to you so clever. You say, "a symptom of the end." The end of *what*, I ask you?

MR. Z. Naturally the end of what we have been talking about. As you remember, we have been discussing the history of mankind, and that his- torical "process" which has doubtless been going on at an ever-increasing rate, and which I am certain is nearing its end.

LADY. *C'est la fin du monde, n'est-ce pas?* The argument is becoming a most extraordinary one!

GENERAL. At last we have got to the most interesting subject.

PRINCE. You will not, of course, forget Anti- Christ either.

MR. Z. Certainly not. He takes the most prominent place in what I have to say.

PRINCE (*to Lady*). Pardon me, please. I am now exceedingly busy on very urgent matters. I am very anxious to hear the discussion on this most fascinating subject, but, I am sorry to say, I must return home.

GENERAL. Return home? And what about whist ?

POLITICIAN. I had a presentiment from the very first day that some villainy or other was being pre- pared. Where religion is involved, never expect any good. *Tantum religio potuit suadere malorum.*

PRINCE. No villainy is about to be perpetrated. I will try to come back at nine o'clock, but now I positively have no time.

LADY. Why this sudden urgency? How is it that you didn't inform us of those important matters before? No, I refuse to believe you. Candidly, it is Anti-Christ that has scared you, isn't it?

PRINCE. I heard so frequently yesterday that politeness is everything, that under the spell of this theory I have ventured for the sake of politeness to tell a lie. Now I see that I am wrong, and I tell you frankly that though I am busy with many important matters, I am leaving this discussion mainly because I consider it a sheer waste of time to discuss things which can be of interest only to Papooses and such like.

POLITICIAN. Your very polite sin is now expiated, it seems.

LADY. Why get cross? If we are stupid, en- lighten us. Take me, for instance. You see, I am not cross with you for having been called a Papoose. Why, even Papooses may have correct ideas. God makes infants wise. But if it is so difficult for you to hear about Anti-Christ, we'll agree on this: Your villa is only a few steps from here. You go home to your work now, and towards the end of the discussion come back after Anti-Christ. . . .

PRINCE. Very well. I will come, with pleasure. (*After the Prince had left the company.*) GENERAL (*laughing*). " The cat knows whose meat he's eaten up."[15]

LADY. What, you think our Prince is an Anti- Christ?

GENERAL. Well, not personally, not he per- sonally; it will be a long time before he gets as far as that. But he is on the right track, all the same. As it is said in the Gospel of St. John: " You have heard, my little ones, that Anti-Christ is coming, and there are many Anti-Christs now." So, one of these "many . . ."

LADY. One may find oneself amongst the "many" against one's wish. God will not punish him for that. He simply has been led astray. He knows that he will not discover his own gunpowder, whilst wearing a fashionable coat is an honour after all. It is only as if one were transferred from the Army to the Guards. For a big General it makes no difference, but for a small officer it is very flattering.

POLITICIAN. The psychology is very sound. Yet I am unable to see why he should have become so angry when Anti-Christ was mentioned. Take me, for instance. I have no faith whatever in things mystical, and so it does not annoy me. On the contrary, it rather excites my curiosity from a general human standpoint: I know that for many it is something very serious; it is clear, then, that in this matter some

---

[15] A Russian proverb. (Translator.)

side of human nature has found its expression, a side which is possibly atrophied in my consciousness, but which does not cease to pre- serve its objective interest even for me. I, for instance, am a very bad judge of paintings: I cannot draw even a straight line or a circle, nor am I able to perceive what is bad and what is good in the works of painters. Yet I am interested in the art of painting from the standpoint of general education and general aesthetics.

LADY. It is difficult to be offended at such a harm- less thing as art. But religion, for instance, you hate with all your heart, and only just now you quoted some Latin curse against it.

POLITICIAN. A curse! Good gracious! In the words of my favourite poet Lucretius, I merely blamed religion for its bloodstained altars and the cries of the human beings sacrificed upon them. I can hear an echo of this bloodthirstiness in the gloomy-intolerant utterances of the companion who has just left us. Still, religious ideas *per se* interest me very much—amongst others this idea of the "Anti-Christ." Unfortunately, all I have been able to read on this subject is confined to the book by Renan, and he considers the question only in relation to historical evidence, which in his opinion points indubitably to Nero. But this is not sufficient.

We know that the idea of "Anti-Christ" was held by the Jews long before the time of Nero—and was applied by them to the King Antiochus Epiphanes. It is still believed in by the Russian "old-believers," so there must be some truth in it, after all.

GENERAL. The leisure your Excellency enjoys affords you every opportunity for the discussion of such high matters. But our poor Prince employs so much of his time in preaching evangelical morals that he is naturally prevented from pondering on Christ or Anti-Christ: even for his whist he cannot get more than three hours a day.

LADY. You are very severe on him, General. It is true that all of his crowd seem unnatural, but then they look so miserable, too : you won't find in them any joy, good humour, or placidity. Yet is it not said in the Gospels that Christianity is the joy of the Holy Ghost?

GENERAL. The position is, indeed, very difficult: to be lacking in Christian spirit, and yet to pass themselves off as true Christians.

MR. Z. As Christians *par excellence* without pos- sessing what constitutes the real excellence of Christianity.

GENERAL. It seems to me that this pitiful position is just the position of Anti-Christ, which for the more clever and sensitive is made more burdensome by the knowledge they have that no luck can help them.

MR. Z. In any case it is beyond doubt that the

Anti-Christianity which, according to the Bible, both in the Old and the New Testaments, marks the clos- ing scene of the tragedy of history, will be not a mere infidelity to or a denial of Christianity, or materialism or anything similar to it, but that it will be a religious imposture, when the name of Christ will be arrogated by such forces in mankind which are in practice and in their very essence alien, and even inimical, to Christ and His Spirit.

GENERAL. Naturally so. The Devil would not be what he is if he played an open game!

POLITICIAN. I am afraid, however, lest all the Christians should prove mere impostors, and there- fore, according to you, mere Anti-Christs. The only exception will perhaps be the unconscious masses of the people, in so far as such are still exist- ing, and a few originals like yourselves, ladies and gentlemen. In any case, there can be no doubt that the name of "Anti-Christ" justly applies to those persons, who here in France, as well as in our country, are particularly busy about Christianity, make of it their special occupation, and consider the name of Christian some sort of monopoly or privi- lege of their own. In our time such people fall in one of the two categories equally alien, I hope, to the spirit of Christ. They are either mad slaugh- terers ready to revive forthwith the terrors of the inquisition and to organise religious massacres after the style of those "pious" abbes and "brave" "Catholic" officers who recently gave vent to their feelings on the occasion of celebrating some de- tected swindler.[16] Or they may be the new ascetics and celibates who have discovered virtue and con- science as some new America, whilst losing at the same time their inner truthfulness and common sense. The first cause in one a moral repulsion. The second make one yawn for very boredom.

GENERAL. This is quite true. Even in the past, Christianity was unintelligible to some and hateful to others. But it remained to our time to make it either repulsive or so dull that it bores men to death. I can imagine how the Devil rubbed his hands and laughed until his stomach ached when he learned of this success. Good gracious me!

LADY. Well, is this Anti-Christ as you understand him?

MR. Z. Oh, no! Some signs indicating his nature are given here, but he himself is still to come.

LADY. Then will you explain in the simplest way possible what the matter really is?

MR. Z. As to simplicity, that cannot, I am afraid, be guaranteed. It is difficult to assume true sim- plicity whenever you wish. But a sham, artificial, false simplicity—nothing can be worse than that. There is an old saying which was often repeated by a friend of mine, now dead: *"Many a simplicity is hurtful"*

LADY. This is not so simple either.

---

[16] The Politician obviously refers here to the public sub- scription opened in commemoration of the "suicide" Henry, in which one French officer stated that he subscribes in the hope of seeing a new St. Bartholomew massacre; another officer wrote that he was looking forward to an early execu- tion of all Protestants, Freemasons, and Jews, whilst an abbé confessed that he lived by anticipation of that glorious time when the skin stripped off the Huguenots, the Masons, and the Jews will be used for making cheap carpets, and when he will, as a good Christian, always tread such a carpet with his feet. These statements, amongst tens of thousands of others in a similar vein, were published in the paper, *La Libre Parole*. (Author.)

GENERAL. I believe it is the same as the popular proverb: "Some simplicities are worse than thefts."

MR. Z. You've guessed it!

LADY. Now I understand it too.

MR. Z. It is a pity, though, that one cannot ex- plain all about Anti-Christ by proverbs.

LADY. Then explain as best you can.

MR. Z. Very well then. In the first place, tell me whether you recognise the existence and the power of evil in the world?

LADY. One would prefer not to recognise it, but one can hardly help doing so. Death alone would make one believe it: for death is an evil one cannot escape. I verily believe that " the last enemy to be destroyed will be death"—but before it is de- stroyed, it is clear that evil is not only strong in itself but even much stronger than good.

MR. Z. And what is your opinion?

GENERAL. I have never shut my eyes before bullets and shells, and shall certainly not do so when faced with subtle questions. Certainly, evil is as real as good. There is God, but there is the Devil also—of course, so long as God tolerates him.

POLITICIAN. As for myself, I shall abstain from a definite answer for a time. My view does not go deeply to the root of the matter, and that side of it which is clear to me I explained as best I could yesterday. But I am interested to know what other people think of it. I can understand perfectly well the Prince's mode of thought. In other words, I understand that there is no real thought in his case at all, but only a naked pretension *qui n'a ni rime ni raison*. The positive religious view, however, is much more intelligent and more interesting. Only up to the present all my acquaintance with it was confined to its official form, which affords me very little satisfaction indeed. I should be very pleased to hear, instead of the vapourings of mealy-mouthed parsons, the natural human word.

MR. Z. Of all the stars that rise on the mental horizon of a man who carefully reads our Sacred Books, I think there is none so clear, illuminating, and startling as that shining in the words, "Thinkest thou that I come to bring peace on Earth? I come not to bring peace, but a sword." He came to bring *truth* to the earth, and truth, like good, before everything else *divides*.

LADY. This needs to be explained. If you are right, why is it that Christ is called the Prince of Peace, and why did He say that peacemakers will be called the children of God?

MR. Z. And you are so kind that you wish me also to obtain that higher distinction by making peace between contradictory texts?

LADY. I do wish it.

MR. Z. Then, please note that the only way of making peace between them is by distinguishing between the good or true peace and the bad or wrong peace. This distinction was clearly pointed out by Him who brought to us the true peace and the good enmity: "My peace I leave with you, My peace I give unto you. Not as the world giveth, give I unto you." There is therefore the good peace—the peace of Christ, resting on the *division* which Christ came to bring to the world, namely, the division be- tween good and evil, between truth and untruth. There is also the bad peace—the peace of the world which endeavours to blend or to unite together ex- ternally elements which internally are at war with one another.

LADY. But how can you show the difference be- tween the good and the bad peace?

MR. Z. In very much the same way as the General did when, the other day, he remarked in a jocular way that one may have a good peace like that, for instance, concluded by the treaties of Nistadt and Kuchuk-Kainardji. Beneath this joke lies hidden a serious and significant meaning. As in the political struggle, so in the spiritual one; the good peace is that concluded when the object of the war is accomplished.

LADY. And what is the object of the war between good and evil? I am not sure if it is even necessary for them to wage a war with each other, or if such a thing as an actual conflict is possible between them— *corps* à *corps*! In the ordinary war, when one side becomes the stronger, the opposing side also looks for reinforcements, and the struggle has to be decided by pitched battles, with guns and bayonets. You will find nothing like this in the struggle between good and evil. In this struggle, when the good side becomes stronger, the bad side immediately weakens, and the struggle never leads on to a real battle. So that all this must be taken only in a metaphorical sense. Thus it is one's duty to foster the growth of good in man. Evil will then diminish as a matter of course.

MR. Z. In other words, you believe that it is enough for kind people to grow still kinder, and that then wicked people would go on losing their malice until finally they become as kind as the others.

LADY. I believe that is so.

MR. Z. But do you know of any case when the kindness of a kind man made the wicked man also kind, or at least less wicked?

LADY. No, candidly I do not. Neither have I seen or heard of such cases.... But, pardon me, is not what you have said just now similar to what you were discussing with the Prince the other day? That even Christ, however kind He was, could not convert the souls of Judas and the impenitent thief? You will not forget that the Prince has still to answer this, will you?

MR. Z. Well, since I don't believe the Prince to be Anti-Christ, I have little faith in his coming, and still less in his theological presence of mind. How- ever, in order to relieve our discussion from the burden of this unsolved question, I will state the objection which the Prince should make from his *standpoint*. "Why did not Christ regenerate the wicked souls of Judas and Co. by the power of His goodness?" For the simple reason, the answer would run, that it was a dark time, and only a few choice souls reached that degree of moral develop- ment which allows of an adequate response to the inner power of truth. And Judas and Co. were too "backward" for that. Furthermore, Jesus Himself said to His disciples: "Deeds which I do, you will do also, and even *more* than this you *will do*" It follows that at a higher stage of moral progress in mankind, such as is reached at the present time, the true disciples of Christ are able by the power of their kindness, and by forcibly refusing to resist evil, to perform moral miracles surpassing even those which were possible eighteen centuries ago....

GENERAL. Just a moment! If they are able to perform miracles, why don't they? Or have you seen some of these new miracles? Even now, after "eighteen centuries of moral progress in Christian consciousness," our Prince is still unable to en- lighten my dark soul. Just as I was a barbarian before I met him, so I remain. I am just what I have always been. After God and Russia, what I love most is military work in general, and the artillery in particular. And in my lifetime I have met not only our Prince, but other non- resisters as well, and some perhaps even stronger than he.

MR. Z. Why assume such a personal attitude? And why hold me responsible? I only produced on behalf of your absent opponent a text from the Gospels which he forgot.

LADY. Now I think I must defend our poor Prince. If he wanted to be really clever, he would say to the General: "I and those whom you have found to hold my views consider ourselves to be true disciples of Christ, but only in the sense of a general trend of thought and action, and not of having any greater power of doing good. But we are certain that there are, or will shortly be somewhere, Chris- tians-more perfect than we, and they will be able to enlighten even your obscurity."

MR. Z. This answer would, no doubt, be very ingenious, as it would introduce an unknown quan- tity. But it can hardly be called serious. Suppose they say, or should say: "We can do nothing greater than what Christ did, nothing even equal to it, nothing even which falls little short of it"? What conclusion could be drawn from this according to the rules of sound logic?

GENERAL. Only one, it seems, namely, that the words of Christ: "You will do what I did, and even more than this," were addressed not to these gentle- men, but to other persons who do not resemble them in the least.

LADY. Yet it is possible to imagine that some man will carry out Christ's commandment about loving his enemies and forgiving those who do wrong to him. And then he will, with the help of Christ Himself, acquire the power to convert wicked souls into good ones.

MR. Z. Not so long ago an experiment was tried in this direction, and not only did it not realise its object, but it actually proved the very opposite to what you are supposing now. There lived a man whose kindness knew no bounds. He not only forgave every wrong done to him, but for every evil returned deeds of kindness. Now what do you suppose happened? Do you think he stirred the soul of his enemy and regenerated him morally? Alas! he only exasperated the evil spirit of the villain, and died miserably by his hand.

LADY. What case are you talking about? What man was he? Where and when did he live?

MR. Z. Not so long ago, and in St. Petersburg. I fancy I knew him. His name is M. Delarue, a court chamberlain.

LADY. I have never heard of him, though I think I can count on my fingers all the leading people of the city.

POLITICIAN. Neither can I recollect him. But what is the story about this chamberlain?

MR. Z. It has been splendidly told in an unpub- lished poem by Count Alexis Tolstoy.

LADY. Unpublished? Then it is sure to be a farce. What can it have to do with the serious problems we are discussing?

MR. Z. I can assure you, madame, that, farcical though it is in its form, it contains a very serious story, and, what is more to the point, one true to life. At any rate, the actual relationship between kindness and wickedness in human life is portrayed in these amusing verses with a much greater skill than I could ever show in my serious prose. Moreover, I have not the slightest doubt that when the heroes of some worldwide popular novels, skilfully and seriously tilling the psychological mould, have become a mere literary recollection for book-lovers, this farce, which in an exaggerated and wildly cari- catured form plumbs the very depth of the moral problem, will retain all its artistic and philosophic truth.

LADY. I don't believe in your paradoxes. You are seized with the spirit of contradiction, and wil- fully brave public opinion.

MR. Z. I should probably have "braved" it had it really existed. Still, I am going to tell you the story of court chamberlain Delarue, since you do not know it, and I happen to remember it by heart :

THE END OF HISTORY

The impious assassin struck with a dagger
The great Delarue
In the breast: the other bowed, uncov'ring politely,
And said: "How d'you do!"
The villain plunged again more deeply the dagger,
Far as he could:
And smiling still the stabbed man murmured: "Your weapon's
Remarkably good."
The villain next the right of the other attacking,
Him wounds in the chest;
Delarue at him a finger shaking in fun says,
"How naughty a jest!"
And now in frenzy wild the villain all over
With wounds ill to see
Disfigures the other's body. Delarue: "How time's flying!
Will you stay to tea?"
The villain knelt and sobbed and cried, asking pardon,
Disliking the scene.
"For God's sake, man, get up from the floor!" Delarue cries.
"It isn't too clean."

The villain lies at his feet repentant and grieving,
Confessing his wrong:
Delarue the prostrate man upraises with arms that
Are loving and strong.
"I see you weep. For what? No use in bewailing
A trifle, my dear sir!
I'll speak the Tsar on your behalf. He'll on you
A pension confer.
The ribbon of Stanislaus shall deck your bosom soon—
Does that make you vain?—
I can secure these things, as having the Tsar's ear,
His chief Chamberlain.

Or would you care to wed my daughter, my Mary?
If that is your desire
Ten thousand pounds in notes I will on you settle,
A gift from her sire.
And now, I pray, accept from me this portrait here,
If you'll be so kind:
A token, showing love for you. It isn't framed—
I know you won't mind."
The villain's face grew evil now and sarcastic:
"Is this then my fate,
To owe my life and all I have to a man who
With love repays hate? "
The lofty spirit thus the base aye discovers,
Reveals its disgrace.
Assassins may forgive the gift of a portrait;
Not pension and place.
The fires of envy smoulder in his vile heart's depths,
Dark altars of shame;
And while as yet the ribbon's new on his shoulder,
They burst into flame.
New filled with malice devilish he sets his dagger
In venom to steep;
And from behind the back of Delarue he deals him
A blow sure and deep.
His pains forbidding him to sit, on the floor low
Poor Delarue lies.
The villain flies upstairs, and here poor Mary falls
Despoiled as his prize.
The villain Tambov fled to as Governor there
Is justly esteemed;
And later, in Moscow, as Senator, worthy honour high,
Is by all men deemed;
And soon he attains to an honourable membership
In Council of State;

Oh ! what a good lesson this story teaches us!
Oh! what a fate!

LADY. Oh, how sweet it is, how sweet! I never anticipated anything so delightful!

POLITICIAN. Very fine indeed. Some expressions are real metrical feats.

MR. Z. But note how true to life all this is. Delarue is not a specimen of that "purified virtue" which one never meets in nature. He is a real man with all the human weaknesses. He is vain (" I am a chamberlain," he says) and fond of money (he has managed to save ten thousand pounds); whilst his fantastic immunity from the stabs of the villain's dagger is, of course, merely an obvious symbol of his infinitely good humour, invincible, even insensi- tive to all wrongs—a trait also to be met with in life, though comparatively seldom. Delarue is not a personification of virtue, but a naturally kind- hearted man, in whom kindness overpowered all his bad qualities, driving them to the surface of his soul and revealing them there in the form of inoffensive weaknesses. The "villain" also is not the conven- tional essence of vice, but the normal mixture of good and bad qualities. The evil of envy, however, rooted itself in the very depth of his soul and forced out all the good in him to the *epidermis* of the soul, so to speak, where the kindness became a sort of very active but superficial sentimentality. When Delarue replies to a number of offensive actions with polite words and with an invitation to tea, the villain's sentimentality is greatly moved by these acts of gentleness, and he descends to a climax of repentance. But when later the chamberlain's civility is changed into the sincere sympathy of a deeply good-natured man, who retaliates upon his enemy for the evil done, not with the seeming kindness of nice words and gestures, but by the actual good of practical help—when, I say, Delarue shows interest in the life of his enemy, is willing to share with him his fortune, to secure for him an official post, and even to provide him with family happi- ness, then this real kindness, penetrating into the deeper moral strata of the villain, reveals his inner moral emptiness, and when it reaches the very bottom of his soul it arouses the slumbering croco- dile of envy. It is not the kindness of Delarue that excites the envy of the villain—as you have seen, he can also be kind, and when he cried, pitifully wringing his hands, he doubtless was conscious of this. What did excite his envy was the—for him— unattainable infinite vastness and *simple seriousness* of that kindness:

"Assassins may forgive the gift of a portrait;

Not pension and place."

Is it not realistic? Do we not see this in everyday life? One and the same moisture of vivifying rain causes the development of healing powers in some herbs and of poison in others. In the same way, a real act of kindness, after all, only helps to develop good in the good man and evil in the evil one. If so, how can we—have we even the right to let loose our kind sentiments without choice and distinction? Can we praise the parents for zealously watering from the good can the poisonous flowers growing in their garden, where their children play? I ask you, why was Mary ruined?

GENERAL. With this I fully agree! Had Delarue given a good drubbing to the villain and chucked him out afterwards, the fellow would not have had time for fooling upstairs.

MR. Z. I am prepared to admit that he had the right to sacrifice himself to his kindness. Just as in the past there were martyrs of faith, so in our time I can admit there must be martyrs of kindness. But what, I ask you, should be done with Mary? You know, she is silly and young, and cannot, nor does she wish, to prove anything by her own example. Is it possible, then, not to pity her?

POLITICIAN. I suppose it is not. But I am even more sorry for the fact that Anti-Christ seems to have fled to Tambov with the villain.

MR. Z. Never mind, your Excellency, we'll catch him right enough! Yesterday you were pleased to point out the meaning of history by reference to the fact that natural mankind, at first consisting of a great number of more or less savage races, alien to each other, partly ignorant of each other, partly actually engaged in mutual hostilities that this mankind gradually evolves from within itself its best and most educated part the civilised or Euro- pean world, which ever grows and spreads until it embraces all other groups lagging behind in this historical development, and blends them into one peaceful and harmonious international whole. Estab- lishing a permanent international peace— such is your formula— is it not?

POLITICIAN. Yes, it is. And this formula, in its coming and not far distant realisation, will stand for a much greater achievement in the real progress of culture than it may seem to do at present. Merely reflect on what an amount of evil will die an inevit- able death, and what an amount of good will appear and grow, owing to the very nature of things. What great powers will be released for productive work, what progress will be seen in science and art, industry and trade!

MR. Z. And do you include in the coming achieve- ments of culture a total extinction of diseases and death?

POLITICIAN. Of course . . . to some extent. Quite a good deal has already been done in the way of sanitation, hygienics, antiseptics . . . organo-thera- peutics . . .

MR. Z. Don't you think that these undeniable successes in the positive direction are fully counter- balanced by as little doubtful an increase of neuro- pathic and psychopathic symptoms of the degenera- tion that accompanies the advance of culture?

POLITICIAN. What criteria have we for estimating these?

MR. Z. At any rate, it is absolutely certain that though the *plus* may grow, the minus grows as well, and the result obtained is something very near to nil. This is so far as diseases are concerned. And as to death, it seems nothing but *nil* has ever been obtained in the progress of culture.

POLITICIAN. But the progress of culture never sets before itself such an objective as the extinction of death.

MR. Z. I know it does not. And for this reason it cannot itself be rated very high. Just suppose I know for certain that I myself and all that is dear to me are to disappear for ever. Would it not in such a case be quite immaterial to me whether some- where in the world certain races are righting with each other, or whether they live in peace; whether they are civilised or savage, polite or impolite?

POLITICIAN. Well, it would be, no doubt, from the standpoint of pure egotism.

MR. Z. Why only of egotism? Pardon me, it would be immaterial from any point of view. Death equalises everything, and in face of it egotism and altruism are equally senseless.

POLITICIAN. Let it be so. But the senselessness of egotism does not prevent us from being egotists. Similarly, altruism, so far as it is possible at all, can do quite well without any good reasons, and all your argument about death does not touch it in any way. I am aware that my children and grandchildren are destined to die, but this does not interfere with my efforts to ensure their well-being just as much as if it were to be permanent. I exert myself for their benefit because, in the first place, I love them, and it gives me a moral satisfaction to devote my life to them. "I find taste in it." It is as clear as daylight.

LADY. It is all right so long as everything goes right, though even then the thought of death some- times comes to your head. But what satisfaction and what taste can you get when all sorts of mishaps begin to happen to your children? It is just like waterflowers on a quagmire: you get hold of one and go to the bottom yourself.

MR. Z. Apart from this, you can and must think of your children and grandchildren, *quand meme*, for yourself, without solving or even attempting to solve the question whether your efforts can do them a real and final good. You take trouble about them, not for the sake of any definite object, but because you love them so dearly. A mankind which is not yet in existence cannot excite such love, and here the question put by our intellect as to the *final* meaning or the object of our cares acquires its full importance. If the answer to this question is death, if the final result of your progress and your culture is but the death of one and all, it is then clear that every kind of activity for the cause of progress and civilisation is for no purpose and has no sense. (*Here Mr.*

Z. interrupted his speech, and all those present turned their heads to the gate which clicked, and for a few seconds they remained in attitudes of inquiry. There they saw the Prince, who had entered the garden and was walking with uneven steps towards them)

LADY. Oh! And we have not even started the discussion about the Anti-Christ.

PRINCE. It makes no difference. I have changed my mind, as I think I should not have shown an ill-feeling to the errors of my neighbours before I had heard their plea.

LADY (*in a triumphant voice to the General*). You see! What will you say now?

GENERAL (*sharply*). Nothing!

MR. Z. You have arrived just in time. We are discussing the question whether it is worth while to trouble about progress if we know that the end of it is always death for every man, be he a savage or the highly educated European of the future. What have your theories to say to this?

PRINCE. The true Christian doctrine does not even admit of stating the question in this fashion. The solution of this problem as given in the Gospels "found its most striking and forceful expression in the parable of the Husbandmen. The husbandmen came to imagine that the garden, to which they had been sent to work for their lord, was their own property; that everything that was in the garden was made for them; and that the only thing they had to do was to enjoy their life in that garden, while giving no thought to its lord, and killing everybody who dared to remind them of his existence and of their duties towards him. Like those husbandmen, so nearly all people in our time live in the absurd belief that they themselves are the lords of their life and that it has been given them for their enjoyment. The absurdity of this is obvious. For if we have been sent here, this was done at someone's behest and for some purpose. We have, however, decided that we are like mushrooms: that we were born and now live only for our own pleasure; and it is clear that it is as bad for us as it would be bad for the workman who does not carry out his master's will. But the master's will found its expression in the teaching of Christ. Let people only carry out this teaching, and the Kingdom of God will be estab- lished on earth and men will obtain the greatest good that they are capable of securing. All is in that. Seek for the Kingdom of God, and His truth and the rest will come to you of itself. We seek for *the rest* and do not find it; and not only do we not establish the Kingdom of God, but we actually destroy it"[17] by our various States, armies, courts, universities, and factories.

GENERAL (*aside*). Now the machine has been wound up.

POLITICIAN (*to the Prince*). Have you finished?

PRINCE. Yes, I have.

POLITICIAN. I must tell you that your solution of the question seems to me absolutely incompre- hensible. You seemingly argue about something, try to prove and to explain something, desire to convince us of something, and yet what you say is all a series of arbitrary and mutually disconnected statements. You say, for instance: "If we have been sent here, this was done at someone's behest and for some purpose." This seems to be your main idea. But what is it? Where did you learn that we have been sent here for a definite purpose? Who told you this? That we exist here on the earth— this is an indisputable fact; but that our existence is some sort of ambassadorship—this you have no ground whatever for asserting. When, for example, I was in my younger days an ambassador, I knew this for certain, as I also knew by whom and for what I was sent—firstly, because I had incontestable documents stating it; secondly, because I had a personal audience of the late Emperor, Alexander II., and received in person instructions from his Imperial Majesty; and, thirdly, because every quarter I was paid ten thousand roubles in sterling gold. Now, if instead of all that some stranger had come up to me in the street and said that I was made an ambassador to be sent to some place, for some purpose or other—well, I should at once have looked round to see if I could find a policeman who would protect me from a maniac, capable, perhaps, even of committing an assault on my person. As regards the present case, you will admit that you have no

---

[17] Quotation from Tolstoy. (Translator.)

incontestable documents from your sup- posed Lord, that you have had no personal audience with Him and that no salary is being paid to you. And you call yourself an ambassador! Why, not only yourself, but even everybody in existence you have declared to be either an ambassador or a hus- bandman. Have you any right to make such statements? Or any ground? No, I refuse to understand it. It seems to me a kind of rhetorical improvisation *tres mal inspireée d'ailleurs*.

LADY. Again pretending ignorance! How bad of you! You understand only too well that the Prince did not think of refuting your atheism, but simply stated the commonly accepted Christian opinion that we all depend on God and are obliged to serve Him.

POLITICIAN. No, I cannot understand a service without a salary. And if it proves that the salary here is one and the same for everybody death, well then, I present my compliments. . . .

LADY. But you will die in any case, and nobody will ask for your consent.

POLITICIAN. It is precisely this very "in any case" that proves that life is not service, and that if no consent of mine is required for my death, just as for my birth, then I prefer to see in death and life what there is actually in them, that is a natural necessity, and not some imaginary service to some unknown master. So my conclusion is this: live, while you live, and endeavour to live in the best and most intelligent manner; and the condition of good and intelligent life is peaceful culture. However, I am of the opinion that even on the basis of the Christian doctrine the sham solution of the problem, sug- gested by the Prince, will not stand the slightest criticism. But let the others, more competent than myself, speak of this.

GENERAL. Of course, it is not a solution at all. It is merely a verbal way of getting round the ques- tion. Just as if I took a map and, having sur- rounded with my pencilled battalions an enemy's pencilled fortress, imagined then that I actually took the actual fortress. Things of this kind did really happen, you know, as the popular soldiers' song tells :

Of this month scarce three days were spent

When devil-driven forth we went
To occupy the hill-tops.

Came Princes, Counts, to see us chaps,
What time surveyors made great maps
On sheets of fair white paper.

On paper, hills are smooth, no doubt,
For all the ravines they'd left out!
'Twas these we had to walk on!

And the result of that is also known:—

At last we to the summit got
And counted up our little lot;
Of all our regiments there were not
A couple of battalions!

PRINCE. No, it is beyond me. And is this all you can answer to what I have been saying here?

GENERAL. In what you have been saying here one thing seemed to me particularly obscure your re- marks about mushrooms, that these live for their own enjoyment. My impression has always been that they live for the enjoyment of those who like to eat mushrooms with cream or in mushroom-pies. Now, if your Kingdom of God on earth leaves death as it is, it follows then that men, quite independently of their will, live, and will live, in your Kingdom of God just like mushrooms—and not those jolly imaginary mushrooms, but the actual ones which are cooked in a pan. The end of man in this our earthly Kingdom of God will be also to be eaten up by death.

LADY. The Prince didn't say so.

GENERAL. Neither so, nor otherwise. But what is the reason of such a reticence concerning the most important point?

MR. Z. Before we raise this question, I would like to learn the source of this parable in which you, Prince, expressed your view. Or is it entirely your own production?

PRINCE. My own production? Why, it is taken from the Gospels!

MR. Z. Oh, no, no, you are surely wrong! You won't find this parable in any of the Gospels.

LADY. Good gracious! What are you trying to confuse the Prince for? You know that there is a parable about husbandmen in the Gospels; surely you do.

MR. Z. There is something resembling it in the external story, but entirely different in the actual events and their meaning, which is immediately thereafter pointed out.

LADY. Oh, no, surely not! I think it is exactly the same parable. Oh, you are trying to be too clever, I notice—I don't trust a single word of yours.

MR. Z. There is no need for it: the book is in my pocket. (*Here Mr. Z got out a small pocket edition of the Gospels and began turning over the pages.*) The parable of the husbandman can be found given by three evangelists: Saints Matthew, Mark, and Luke, but all of them state it in very much the same form. It will, therefore, be sufficient to quote it from the more elaborate Gospel of St. Luke. It is in Chapter XX., in which the last sermon of Christ to the people is given. The drama was nearing its end, and it is now narrated (end of Chapter XIX. and beginning of Chapter XX.) how the enemies of Christ—the party of chief priests and scribes made an open and decisive attack on Him, demanding publicly that He should state His authority and explain by what right and in virtue of what power He was acting. But I think I had better read it to you. (*Reads.*) "And He taught daily in the Temple. But the chief priests and the scribes and the chief of the people sought to destroy Him. And could not find what they might do ; for all the people were very attentive to hear Him. And it came to pass, that on one of those days, as He taught the people in the Temple, and preached the Gospel, the chief priests and the scribes came upon Him with the elders. And spake unto Him, saying: Tell us, by what authority doest Thou these things? or who is He that gave Thee this authority? And He answered and said unto them, I will also ask you one thing, and answer Me: The baptism of John, was it from Heaven or of men? And they reasoned with themselves, saying, If we shall say, From Heaven, He will say, Why then believed ye Him not? But and if we say, Of men, all the people will stone us; for they be persuaded that John was a prophet. And they answered, that they could not tell whence it was: And Jesus said unto them, Neither tell I you by what authority I do these things. . . ."

LADY. And why do you read all this? It was quite right of Christ not to answer when he was worried by these men. But what has it to do with the husbandmen?

MR. Z. A little patience: it all leads to the same thing. Besides, you are mistaken when you say that Christ did not answer. He answered most definitely —and even doubly: quoted such a witness of His authority as the questioners dared not reject, and next proved that they themselves had no proper authority or right over Him, as they acted only out of fear of the people, afraid for their lives, adapting themselves to the opinions of the mob. But real authority is that which does not follow others, but itself leads them forward. Fearing and obeying the people, these men revealed that the real authority had deserted them and belonged to the people. It is to these latter that Christ now addresses Himself in order to accuse them of resisting Him. In this accusation of the unworthy leaders of the Jewish nation for their resistance to the Messiah—there lies all the story of the gospel parable of the husbandmen, as you will presently see for yourself. (*Reads*): "Then began He to speak to the people this parable: A certain man planted a vineyard, and let it forth to husbandmen, and went into a far country for a long time. And at the season he sent a servant to the husbandmen, that they should give him of the fruit of the vineyard: but the husband- men beat him, and sent him away empty. And again he sent another servant, and they beat him also, and entreated him shamefully, and sent him away empty. And again he sent a third: and they wounded him also, and cast him out. Then said the lord of the vineyard, What shall I do? I will send my beloved son: it may be they will reverence him when they see him. But when the husbandmen saw him, they reasoned among themselves, saying, This is the heir: come, let us kill him, that the inheritance may be ours. So they cast him out of the vineyard, and killed him. What, therefore, shall the lord of the vineyard do unto them? He shall come and destroy these husbandmen and shall give the vineyard to others. And when they heard it, they said, God forbid. And He beheld them and said, What is this then that is written, The stone which the builders rejected, the same is become the head of the corner? Whosoever shall fall upon that stone shall be broken; but on whomsoever it shall fall, it will grind him to powder. And the chief priests and the scribes that same hour sought to lay hands on Him; for they feared the people: for they perceived that He had spoken this parable against them." About whom, then, and about what, I ask you, was the parable of the vineyard told?

PRINCE. I can't understand what it is you are driving at. The Judean chief priests and scribes felt offended because they were, and knew them- selves to be, the representatives of those wicked lay people of which the parable spoke.

MR. Z. But of what was it they were accused in the parable?

PRINCE. Of not carrying out the true teaching.

POLITICIAN. I think the whole thing is clear enough. The scoundrels lived like mushrooms for their own enjoyment, smoked tobacco, drank spirits, ate slaughtered meat, and even treated their god to it: besides which, they got married, took the chair in the courts, and engaged in warfare.

LADY. Do you really think that it suits your age and position to indulge in such sneering outbursts? Don't listen to him, Prince. We both want to speak seriously. Now tell me this : after all, according to the parable, the husbandmen were destroyed be- cause they had killed the lord's son and heir and this is the main point in the Gospel. Why, then, do you omit it?

PRINCE. I leave it out for the simple reason that it refers to the personal fate of Christ, which, natur- ally, has its own importance and interest, but is, after all, inessential to that which is one and the same for everybody.

LADY. Which is . . . ?

PRINCE. The carrying out of the Gospel teaching, by means of which the Kingdom of God and His justice are attained.

LADY. Just one second: I feel everything is now mixed up in my head. . . . What is it we are talking about? Ah! (*To Mr. Z.*) You have the Gospel in your hand, so you will perhaps tell us what follows the parable in that particular chapter.

MR. Z. (*turning over the pages*]. It is also stated there that it is necessary that those things which be Caesar's should be rendered to Caesar; that the dead will be raised, because God is not a God of the dead, but of the living, and there is further given a proof that Christ is not David's son, but the Son of God. Then the last two verses are against the hypocrisy and vanity of the Scribes.

LADY. You see, Prince, this is also a Gospel teaching; that the State should be recognised in lay matters, that we should believe in the resurrec- tion of the dead, and that Christ is not an ordinary man, but God's Son.

PRINCE. It is impossible to conclude anything from a single chapter, composed no one knows when or by whom.

LADY. Oh, no! This I know even without look- ing up the matter in books, that not only in a single chapter, but in all the four Gospels, a great deal is said both about resurrection and about Christ's

Divinity—particularly in St. John's Gospel, which is even read at funeral services.

MR. Z. As to the uncertainty of the origin of the Gospels, it is now recognised, even by the liberal German critics, that all the four Gospels were com- posed in the time of the Apostles, that is, in the first century.

POLITICIAN. Why, even the thirteenth edition of "*La Vie de Jésus*" [1] I have noticed contains a retractation of what had originally been said about the fourth gospel.

MR. Z. One must not lag behind one's teachers. But the principal difficulty, Prince, is that whatever our four Gospels may be, whenever and by whomso- ever they were composed, there is no other gospel extant more trustworthy and more in agreement with your teaching than this.

GENERAL. Who told you it does not exist? Why, there is the fifth one, which contains nothing of Christ but the *teaching*—about slaughtered meat and military service.

LADY. And you also? You should be ashamed of yourself. Remember that the more you and your civil ally tease the Prince, the more support I shall give him myself. I am sure, Prince, that you want to look upon Christianity from its best side, and that your gospel, though not the same as ours, is similar to the books composed in times gone by: something like " L' Esprit de M. de Montesquieu," "L'Esprit de Fénelon," etc. In the same way, you or your teachers wanted to compose "L'esprit de l'Evangile." It is only a great pity that nobody of your persuasion has done it in a small book, which could be called "*The Spirit of Christianity* according to the teaching of so-and-so." You should have some sort of a catechism, so that we simple folk should not lose the thread in all your variations. One moment we are told that the whole thing is in the Sermon on the Mount; another moment that we must first of all labour in the sweat of our brow in agricultural work—though the Gospel does not say this anywhere. Genesis does, however, in the part where it also speaks of giving birth in pains—this, however, not being a commandment, but only a grievous necessity. Then we are told that we must give everything we have to the poor, and the next moment that we must not give any- thing to anybody, since money is evil, and it is bad to do evil to others, save to ourselves and our family; whilst for the rest we must work. Then again we are told to do nothing but contemplate. Yet again, that the mission of women is to give birth to as many healthy children as possible, and then suddenly that nothing of the kind is necessary. Then that we must not eat meat—this is the first stage, and why the first nobody can tell. We must give up now spirits and smoking, now pancakes. Last comes the objection to military service that all evil is due to it, and that the first duty of a Christian is to refuse doing it; and whoever has not been officially recruited is, of course, holy as he is. Perhaps I am talking nonsense, but this is not my fault—it is absolutely impossible for me to make head or tail of all this.

PRINCE. I also think that we require a sensible summary of the true teaching—I believe it is being prepared now.

LADY. Before it is prepared, tell me briefly what is, in your opinion, the essence of the Gospel.

PRINCE. Surely it is clear enough: it is the great principle of the non-resistance of evil by force.

POLITICIAN. And how do you deduce from this the smoking?

PRINCE. What smoking?

POLITICIAN. Oh, dear me! I ask what connection is there between the principle of the non-resistance of evil and the rules of abstinence from tobacco, wine, meat, and amorous indulgence?

PRINCE. It seems the connection is obvious: all these vicious habits stupefy the man—stifle in him the demands of his intelligence and conscience. This is why soldiers generally go to war in a state of drunkenness.

MR. Z. Particularly to an unsuccessful war. But we may leave this alone. The rule of not resisting evil has its own importance apart from the question whether it justifies ascetic life or does not. According to you, if we do not resist evil by force, evil will immediately disappear. It follows that evil exists only by our resistance or by those measures which we take against it, but has no real power of its own. Properly speaking, there is no evil existing at all, and it appears only owing to our erroneous belief that it does exist and that we begin to act in accordance with the presumption. Isn't it so?

PRINCE. No doubt it is.

MR. Z. But if there is no evil existing in reality how will you explain the startling failure of Christ's cause in history? From your point of view, it has, of course, proved an utter failure, so that no good results can be credited to it, whilst the harm done has undoubtedly far exceeded its good effects.

PRINCE. How is that?

MR. Z. A strange question to ask, to be sure! Well, if you do not understand it we will examine it in a methodical manner. You agree that Christ preached true good in a more clear, powerful, and consistent way than anybody else, didn't He?

PRINCE. Yes, He did.

MR. Z. And the true good is not to resist evil by force, that is to resist imaginary evil, as there is no real evil existing.

PRINCE. Yes.

MR. Z. Christ not only preached, but carried out to the last end the demands of this good by suffering without any resistance the torments of crucifixion. Christ, according to you, died and did not rise. Very well. Thousands of His followers suffered the same. Very well again. But now, what has been the result of it all?

PRINCE. Would you like to see all these martyrs, as a reward of their deeds, crowned by angels with brilliant wreaths and reclining somewhere under the trees in Elysian gardens?

MR. Z. Oh no, there is no need to take it that way. Of course we all, including yourself, I hope, wish all that is best and most pleasant to our neighbours, both living and dead. But the question is not of our wishes, but of what has actually resulted from the preaching and sacrifice of Christ and His followers.

PRINCE. Resulted for whom? For themselves?

MR. Z. What resulted for themselves everybody knows: a painful death. But moral heroes as they were, they willingly accepted it, not in order to get brilliant wreaths for themselves, but to secure true benefit for others, the whole of mankind. Now I ask you, what are the benefits earned by mankind through their martyrdom? In the words of an old saying, "The blood of martyrs is the seed of the Church." In point of fact, it is quite true. But your contention is that the Church has been nothing but the distortion and ruin of true Christianity, which was, as a result, entirely forgotten by man- kind, so that it became necessary to restore every- thing from the very beginning without any guarantee for any greater success; in other words, quite hope- lessly.

PRINCE. Why hopelessly?

MR. Z. Because you have admitted yourself that

Christ and the first generations of Christians gave all their thoughts and sacrificed their lives for their cause, and if, this notwithstanding, nothing resulted from their efforts, what grounds have you then for hoping for any other result? There is only one in- dubitable and permanent end to all such practice of good, the same for those who initiated it, and for those who distorted and ruined it, and for those who have been restoring it. They all, according to you, died in the past, die in the present, will die in the future. And from the practice of good, the preaching of truth, nothing but death ever came, comes, or promises to come. Well, what is the meaning of it all ? Isn't it strange : the non-existent evil always triumphs and the good always falls through to nothingness ?

LADY. Do not evil people die as well ?

MR. Z. Very much so. But the point is that the power of evil is only confirmed by the reign of death, whereas the power of good would, on the contrary, be disproved. Indeed, evil is obviously more powerful than good, and if the obvious is the only thing real, then you cannot but admit that the world is the work of the evil power. How some people, whilst recognising only the obvious reality, and therefore admitting the predominance of evil over good, maintain at the same time that evil does not exist, and that consequently there is no need for fighting it—this passes my understanding, and I expect the Prince to help me in this difficulty.

POLITICIAN. You had better give us first your own method of getting out of it.

MR. Z. It is quite simple. Evil really exists, and it finds its expression not only in the deficiency of good, but in the positive resistance and predomin- ance of the lower qualities over the higher ones in all the spheres of Being. There is an individual evil—when the lower side of men, the animal and bestial passions, resist the better impulses of the soul, *overpowering* them, in the great majority of people. There is a social evil, when the human crowd, individually enslaved by evil, resists the salutary efforts of the few better men and eventually overpowers them. There is, lastly, a physical evil in man, when the baser material constituents of his body resist the living and enlightening power which binds them up together in a beautiful form of organism—resist and break the form, destroying the real basis of the higher life. This is the *extreme* evil, called death. And had we been compelled to recognise the victory of this extreme physical evil as final and absolute, then no imaginary victories of good in the individual and social spheres could be considered real successes. Let us, indeed, imagine that a good man, say Socrates, not only triumphed over his inner forces—the bad passions—but also succeeded in convincing and reforming his social foes, in reconstructing the Hellenic "politeia." Now what would be the use of this ephemeral and superficial victory over evil if it is allowed finally to triumph in the deepest strata of Being over the very foundations of life? Because, both for the reformer and for the reformed there is but one end: death. By what logic would it be possible to appraise highly the moral victories of Socrates' good over the moral microbes of bad passions within him and over the social microbes of the Athenian *agora,* if the real victors would after all be the much worse, baser, and coarser microbes of physical decomposi- tion? Here no moral verbiage will protect you against utter pessimism and despair.

POLITICIAN. We have heard this before. What is your remedy against despair?

MR. Z. Our remedy is one: actual resurrection. We know that the struggle between good and evil is not confined only to soul or society, but is carried on in the deeper spheres of the physical world. We already have recorded in the past one victory of the good power of life—the personal resurrection of One, and we are looking forward to future victories of the congregate resurrection of all. Here even evil is given its reason or the final explanation of its existence in that it serves to enhance the triumph, realisation, and power of good: if death is more powerful than mortal life, resurrection to external life is even more powerful than both of them. The Kingdom of God is the kingdom of life triumphing through resurrection—in which life there lies the real, actual, and final good. In this rests all the power and work of Christ, in this His real love to us and ours to Him; whereas all the other things are only the condition, the path, the preliminary steps. Without the faith in the accomplished resurrection of One, and without cherishing the future resurrec- tion of all men, all talk of some Kingdom of God remains nothing but words, whilst in reality one finds only the Kingdom of Death.

PRINCE. Why that?

MR. Z. Why, because you not only admit with everybody else the *fact* of death as such, that is that men generally died, die, and will die, but you raise this fact to the position of an absolute law, which does not in your opinion permit of a single excep- tion. But what should we call the world in which death for ever has the force of an absolute law but the Kingdom of Death? And what is your Kingdom of God on Earth but an arbitrary and purposeless euphemism for the Kingdom of Death?

POLITICIAN. I also think it is purposeless, because it is wrong to replace a known quantity by an un- known one. Nobody has seen God and nobody knows what His Kingdom may be. But we have all seen the death of men and animals, and we also know that nobody in the world can escape this supreme power of death. What is the good then of replacing this certain "a" by some unknown "x"? Nothing but confusion and temptation for the "little ones" will ever result from such a substitution.

PRINCE. I don't quite understand what it is that we are talking about. Death is, of course, a very interesting phenomenon. One may perhaps call it even a law, in the sense of a phenomenon which is universal amongst earthly beings and unavoidable for any one of them. One may also speak of the absoluteness of this " law," as until now no exception has been authentically recorded. But what material vital importance can all this have for the true Chris- tian teaching which speaks to us, through our con- science, only one thing: that is, what we must and what we must not do *here and now*? It is also obvious that the voice of conscience can refer only to what is in our power to do or not to do. For this reason conscience not only remains silent about death, but cannot be anything else. With all its vastness for our human, worldly feelings and desires, death is not controlled by our will, and cannot there- fore have for us any moral significance. In this relation—and, properly speaking, it is of course the only important one—death is a fact of indifference similar, say, to bad weather. Because I recognise the unavoidable periodical existence of bad weather, and have to suffer from it to a greater or smaller extent, does it follow that for this reason I should, instead of speaking of the Kingdom of God, speak of the kingdom of bad weather?

MR. Z. No, you should not; firstly, because it reigns only in St. Petersburg, and we both come here to the Mediterranean and laugh at it; and, secondly, your comparison is faulty, because even in bad

weather you are able to praise God and feel yourself in His Kingdom, whilst the dead, as you know from the Bible, do not praise God. I agree for these reasons with his Excellency that it is more appro- priate to call this world the Kingdom of Death than the Kingdom of God.

LADY. Why are you arguing all the time about titles? It is so uninteresting. Titles, surely, matter very little. You had better tell me, Prince, what you actually understand by the Kingdom of God and His Truth.

PRINCE. By this I understand the state of men when they act only in accordance with their inner conscience and thus carry out the will of God, which prescribes them nothing but pure good.

MR. Z. The voice of conscience, however, speaks of performing what is due only now and here. Isn't this the view you hold?

PRINCE. You are quite correct.

MR. Z. But does your conscience remain silent about those wicked deeds which you may have com- mitted in your youth in relation to people long since dead?

PRINCE. In such cases the meaning of such reminders would be to warn me against repeating similar deeds now.

MR. Z. Well, it is not exactly so, but we need not argue about it. I would only like to indicate another more incontestable limit of conscience. The moralists have for a long time been comparing the voice of conscience with that genius or demon which accompanied Socrates, warning him against things he should not do, but never giving a positive indication as to what he should do. Precisely the same may be said of conscience.

PRINCE. How is that? Does not conscience sug- gest to me, say, that I should help my neighbour in case of need or danger?

MR. Z. I am very glad to hear this from you. But if you examine such cases thoroughly you will see that the *rôle* of conscience even here remains purely negative: it demands from you only that you should not remain inactive or indifferent in face of your neighbour's need, but as to what and how you should do, this your conscience does not disclose.

PRINCE. Naturally so, because it depends on the circumstances of the case, on my own position, and that of the neighbour whom I must help.

MR. Z. Just so. But weighing and appraising these circumstances is not a matter for conscience, but for your reason.

PRINCE. How can you separate reason from conscience?

MR. Z. You need not separate them, but you must distinguish them. Because just in reality it some- times happens that reason and conscience become not only separated but even opposed to each other. Should they be one and the same thing, how would it then be possible for reason to be used for acts not only foreign to morality, but positively immoral?

And, you know, this does happen. Why, even help can be offered in a way that is approved by reason but is inimical to moral consciousness. For instance, I may give food and drink and show other considera- tion to a needy man in order only to make him an accomplice in a fraud I am preparing, or any other wicked act.

PRINCE. Well, it is, of course, so elementary. But what conclusion do you deduce from it?

MR. Z. The conclusion that if the voice of con- science, however important it may be for the pur- pose of warning and reproving you, does not at the same time give you any positive and practically definite instructions for your conduct; and if, further, our good will requires reason as a subsidiary instru- ment, whereas its services prove rather doubtful as it is equally ready of serving two masters, namely, good and evil, it follows from the above that for carrying out the will of God and attaining to the Kingdom of God, a third thing is necessary besides conscience and reason.

PRINCE. What is it, then?

MR. Z. Briefly it is the *inspiration of good*, or the direct and positive action of the good power itself on us and within us. With this help from above, both reason and conscience become trustworthy assistants of good, and morality itself, instead of the always doubtful " good conduct," is transformed into a real life in the good—into an organic growth and development of the whole man—of his internal and external self, of personality and of society, of nation and of mankind—in order to attain to the vital unity of the risen past with the realising future in that external present of the Kingdom of God which will be, though on the earth, the new Earth, joined in love with the new Heaven.

PRINCE. I have nothing to say against such poetical metaphors, but do not exactly see why men, performing the will of God according to the commandments laid down in the Gospel, are not actuated by what you call "the inspiration of good."

MR. Z. They are not; not only because I do not see in their actions any signs of such an inspiration, of those free and sweeping impulses of love (God does not measure out the spirit He gives to man); nor only because I do not see that joyous and compliant peace arising from possessing those gifts, if even only primary ones, do I fail to see in you the religious inspiration, but because, properly speaking, you yourself recognise its uselessness for you. If good is confined only to carrying out the "rule," there is no room left here for inspiration. Is there? A "rule" is given once and for all, is definite and the same for everybody. He who gave that rule has been dead long since, and, according to you, has never risen to life, so that He has not for us any personal vital existence. Whilst at the same time you see the absolute, primary good, not as a father of light and life, who could breathe light and life straight into you, but as a prudent lord, who sent you, his hirelings, to do the work in his vineyard, while he himself lives somewhere abroad and sends his men to you to bring him his rent.

PRINCE. We did not invent that image arbitrarily,

MR. Z. No, you did not, but you do arbitrarily see in it the highest standard of relations between man and Deity, arbitrarily casting out of the Gospel that which is the most essential part of it : the reference to the son and heir, in which the true standard of relations between man and God is given. You say : the lord, the duties towards the lord, the will of the lord. But I will tell this much: so long as your lord only imposes duties on you and demands from you compliance with his will, I do not see how you can prove to me that he is a true lord and not an impostor.

PRINCE. This is very funny, really! But what if I know in my conscience and reason that the lord's demands express the purest good?

MR. Z. Pardon me, I am not speaking about this. I do not deny that the lord demands good from you. But how does it follow that he is good him- self?

PRINCE. What else could he be?

MR. Z. 'Tis strange to hear it. I, on the con- trary, always thought that the goodness of anybody is proved not by what he wants other people to do, but by his own acts. If this is not clear to you from the standpoint of logic, I will quote you a historical example. The Moscow Tsar, Ivan the Terrible, demanded in his well-known letter to Prince Andreas Kurbsky that the Prince should show the greatest goodness, the loftiest moral heroism, by refusing to resist force and meekly accepting the death of a martyr for the cause of truth. This lord's will was a will of good as far as its demands from the other man was concerned. However, it did not prove in the least that the lord who demanded that good was good himself. It is evident that 'though martyrdom for the cause of truth is of the highest moral value, this does not say anything for Ivan the Terrible, as he in that case was not a martyr, but a torturer.

PRINCE. Perhaps. But what do you want to prove by this?

MR. Z. Simply that until you show me the good- ness of your lord in his own deeds and not in verbal precepts to his employees, I shall stick to my opinion that your distant lord, demanding good from others but doing no good himself, imposing duties but showing no love, never appearing before your eyes but living *incognito* somewhere abroad, is no one else but *the god of this age* . . .

GENERAL. Here it is, this damned incognito!

LADY. Oh, do please say no more of this. How frightful—the Devil must be with us! (*Crosses herself?*)

PRINCE. One might have anticipated that all the time!

MR. Z. I have no doubt, Prince, that you are genuinely erring when you take the clever impostor for real God. The *cleverness* of the impostor is a mitigating circumstance which greatly reduces your own guilt. I myself could not see through it at once. But now I have no doubts of any kind, so you will understand with what feeling I must look at what I consider a deceptive and seductive mask of good.

LADY. Oh, how can you say this. It hurts one's feelings.

PRINCE. I can assure you, madam, it has not hurt mine. The question raised here is a general one, and it presents some considerable interest. It is only strange that my opponent seems to imagine that it can be addressed only to me, and not to him as well. You demand of me that I show you the per- sonal good deeds of my lord that would prove him to be a power of good and not of evil. Very well. But can you show any good deed of your lord which I should be unable to ascribe to mine?

GENERAL. You have already heard of one such deed, by which all the rest stand.

PRINCE. What is it?

MR. Z. The real victory over evil in the real re- surrection. Only this, I repeat, opens the real Kingdom of God, whereas without it you have only the kingdom of death and sin and their creator, the Devil. The resurrection, and not in its metaphorical, but in its literal meaning—here is the testimony of the true God.

PRINCE. Well, if you are pleased to believe in such mythology! But I ask you for facts, which could be proved, and not for your beliefs.

MR. Z. Not so high up, Prince, not so high. We both start from the same belief, or, if you like, mythology, with this difference—that I consistently carry it through to its logical end; whilst you, violat- ing logic, arbitrarily stop at the first stage. After all, you do recognise the power of good and its coming triumph over evil, don't you ?

PRINCE. Most emphatically !

MR. Z. But what is it: a fact or a belief?

PRINCE. A *reasonable* belief.

MR. Z. Let us see if it is so. Reason, as we have been taught at school, amongst other things de- mands that nothing should be accepted without sufficient grounds. Now tell me what sufficient grounds have you, whilst admitting the power that good has in the moral development and perfection of man and mankind, not to admit that power against death?

PRINCE. In my opinion it is for you to answer why you attribute to good some power beyond the limits of the moral sphere.

MR. Z. Oh, I can answer that. If I believe in good and its own power, whilst assuming in the very notion of good its essential and *absolute* superiority, then I am bound by logic to recognise that power as unlimited, and nothing can prevent me from be- lieving in the truth of resurrection, which is *his- torically* testified. However, had you frankly told me from the beginning that Christian *faith* does not concern you, that the subject of it is only mythology for you, then I should naturally have refrained from that animosity to your ideas which I have been un- able to conceal from you. For "fallacy and error are not debited as frauds," and to bear ill-will to people because of their mistaken theoretical notions would disclose one's possession of too feeble a mind, too weak a faith, and too wretched a heart. But everybody really religious, and thereby freed from these extremes of stupidity, cowardice, and heartlessness, must look with real good will at a straightforward, frank, in a word, *honest* opponent and denier of religious truths. It is so rare to meet such a one in our time, and it is even difficult for me to describe to you how greatly I am pleased when I see an open enemy of Christianity. In nearly everyone of them I am inclined to see a future St. Paul, whilst in some of the zealots of Christianity there seem to be looming Judas, the traitor himself. But you, Prince, have now stated your opinion so frankly that I positively refuse to include you amongst the innumerable Judases and little Judases of our time. I can even foresee the moment when I shall feel towards you the same kind disposition of humour which I experience when meeting out- and-out atheists and infidels.

POLITICIAN. Now that we have safely come to the conclusion that neither those atheists and infidels, nor such " true " Christians as our Prince, represent the Anti-Christ, it is time for you to show us his real portrait.

MR. Z. You want rather too much, your Ex- cellency. Are you satisfied, for instance, with a single one of all the innumerable portraits of Christ which, you will admit, have sometimes been made even by artists of genius? Personally, I don't know of a single satisfactory portrait. I believe such is even impossible, for Christ is an individual, unique in His own kind and in the personification of His essence—good. To paint it, a genius will not suffice. The same, moreover, has to be said about Anti- Christ: he is also an individual, singular in com- pleteness and finish, a personification of evil. It is impossible to show his portrait. In Church litera- ture we find only his passport with a description of his general and some special marks . . .

LADY. No; we do not want his portrait, God save us! You had better explain why he himself is wanted, what his mission is, and when he will come.

MR. Z. Well, in this respect I can satisfy you even better than you expect. Some few years ago a fellow-student from the Church Academy, later made a monk, on his death-bed bequeathed to me a manuscript which he valued very much, but did not wish, or was not able, to publish. It was entitled, *"A Short Story of the Anti-Christ."* Though dressed in the form of fiction, as an imaginary fore- cast of the historical future, this paper, in my opinion, gives all that could be said on this subject in accordance with the Bible, with Church tradition, and the dictates of sound sense.

POLITICIAN. Is it the work of our old friend Monk Barsanophius ?

MR. Z. No; this one's name was even more ex- quisite: Pansophius, he was called.

POLITICIAN. Pan Sophius? Was he a Pole?

MR. Z. Not in the least. A son of a Russian parson. If you will permit me to go upstairs to my room I will fetch the manuscript and then read it to you.

LADY. Make haste, make haste! See that you don't get lost!

(*While Mr. Z. was out, the company left their seats and walked in the garden?*)

POLITICIAN. I wonder what it may be: is it my eyesight that is getting weak, or is something taking place in nature? I notice that in no season, in no place, does one see those bright clear days which formerly used to be met with in every climate. Take to-day: there is not a single cloud, and we are far from the sea, and yet everything seems to be tinged with something subtle and imperceptible, which, though small, destroys the full clearness of things. Do you notice this, General?

GENERAL. It is many a year since I began to notice it.

LADY. Last year I also began to notice, and not only in the air, but in the soul as well, that even there the "full clearness," as you style it, is no longer to be found. All is seized with some uneasi- ness and some ill-omened presentiment. I am sure, Prince, you feel it too.

PRINCE. No; I haven't noticed anything par- ticular: the air seems to be as usual.

GENERAL. You are still too young to notice the difference, for you have nothing to compare with. But when one remembers the 'fifties one begins to feel it.

PRINCE. I think the explanation first suggested was the correct one: it is a matter of weak eye- sight.

POLITICIAN. It is hardly open to argument that we are ever growing older. But neither is the earth getting younger, so that our mutual fatigue now begins to show itself.

GENERAL. I think it is even more likely that the Devil, with his tail, is spreading fog over the world. Another sign of the Anti-Christ!

LADY *(pointing to Mr. Z., who was coming down from the terrace]*. We shall learn something about this presently.

(All took their seats, and Mr. Z. began to read his manuscript.")

A SHORT STORY OF THE ANTI-CHRIST.

Pan-Mongolim! The name is savage,
But it pleases my ear immensely,
As if it were full of forebodings
Of the great destiny appointed by God. . . .

LADY. Where is this motto taken from?
MR. Z. I think it is the work of the author himself.
LADY. Well, we are listening.
MR. Z *(reads)*. The twentieth century A.D. was the epoch of the last great wars and revolutions. The greatest of those wars had its remote cause in the movement of *Pan-Mongolism*, which originated in Japan as far back as the end of the nineteenth century. The imitative Japanese, who showed such a wonderful cleverness in copying the external forms of European culture, also assimilated certain Euro- pean ideas of the baser sort. Having learned from the papers and text-books on history that there were in the West such movements as Pan-Hellenism, Pan-Germanism, Pan-Slavism, Pan-Islamism, they proclaimed to the world the great idea of Pan- Mongolism; that is, the unification under their leadership of all the races of Eastern Asia, with the object of conducting a determined warfare against the foreign intruders, that is the Europeans. As in the beginning of the twentieth century Europe was engaged in a

final struggle against the Moslem world, they seized the opportunity to attempt the realisation of their great plan—first, by occupying Korea, then Peking, where, assisted by the revolu- tionary party in China, they deposed the old Manchu dynasty and put in its place a Japanese one. In this the Chinese Conservatives soon acquiesced, as they understood that of two evils the less is the better, and that "family ties make all brothers, whether they wish it or not." The *state* indepen- dence of old China already proved unable to maintain itself, and subjection to the Europeans or the Japanese became inevitable. It seemed clear, however, that the dominance of the Japanese, though it abolished the external forms of the Chinese state organisation (which besides became palpably worth- less), did not interfere with the main foundations of the national life, whereas the dominance of the Euro- pean Powers, which for political reasons supported Christian missionaries, would have threatened the very spiritual basis of China. The national hatred in which the Japanese were formerly held by the Chinese developed at a time when neither one nor the other knew the Europeans, and in consequence this enmity of two kindred nations acquired the character of a family feud and was as unreasonable as it was ridiculous. The Europeans were *unre- servedly* alien, *nothing but* enemies, and their pre- dominance promised nothing that could flatter the national ambition, whilst in the hands of Japan the Chinese saw the tempting bait of Pan-Mongolism, which at the same time made more acceptable to their mind the painful necessity of assimilating the external forms of the European culture. "Will you understand, you obstinate brothers," the Japanese urged them repeatedly, "that we take from the Western dogs their weapons, not because we like them, but so as to beat them with their own devices ? If you come out to join us and accept our practical guidance, we shall soon be able not only to drive out all the white devils from our Asia, but also to conquer their own lands and establish the true Middle Empire all the world over. You are right in your national pride and your contempt for the Europeans, but you should keep these feelings alive not only by dreams, but by sensible actions as well. In these latter we are far in advance of you and have to show you the ways of mutual benefit. If you look around you will see yourselves what little gains you have obtained by your policy of confidence in your- selves and mistrust of us—your natural friends and protectors. You have seen how Russia and England, Germany and France nearly divided you up amongst themselves, and how all your tigerish schemes could show only the harmless end of the serpent's tail." The sensible Chinese found this reasonable, and the Japanese dynasty became firmly established. Its first care was, of course, to create a powerful army and fleet. The greater part of the Japanese troops were brought over to China and served as a nucleus for the new colossal army. The Japanese officers who could speak Chinese proved much more suc- cessful instructors than the dismissed Europeans, whilst the immense population of China, with Man- churia, Mongolia, and Tibet, provided a sufficient supply of good fighting material. It was already possible for the first Emperor of the Japanese dynasty to make a successful test of the power of the new Empire by driving out the French from Tonkin and Siam, and the English from Burma, and by adding to the Middle Empire the whole of Indo-China. His successor, Chinese on his mother's side, combined in himself Chinese cunning and tenacity with Japanese energy, agility, and enter- prise. He mobilised a four-million army in the Chinese Turkestan, and whilst Tsun-li-Yamin, his Prime Minister, was confidentially informing the Russian Ambassador that this army was intended for the invasion of India, the Emperor with his immense forces suddenly invaded Russian Central Asia, and having here raised against us all the population, rapidly crossed the Ural Mountains and overran Eastern and Central Russia with his troops, whilst the Russian armies, mobilised in all haste, were hurrying to meet them from Poland and Lithuania, Kiev and Volhyn, St. Petersburg, and Finland. Having no ready plan of campaign, and being faced with an immense superiority in numbers, the fighting qualities of the Russian armies were sufficient only to allow them honourable defeat. The swiftness of the invasion left them no time for a proper concen- tration, and corps were annihilated one after another in desperate and hopeless battles. The victories of the Mongols also involved tremendous losses, but these were easily made good with the help of all the Asiatic railways, while the Russian Army, two hundred thousand strong, and for some time con- centrated on the Manchurian frontier, made an abor- tive attempt to invade well-defended China. After leaving a portion of his forces in Russia, so that no new armies could be formed in the country, and also to fight the numerous bodies of *franc-tireurs*, the Emperor with three armies crossed the frontiers of Germany. Here the country had had sufficient time to prepare itself, and one of the Mongolian armies met with a crushing defeat. At this time, however, in France the party of belated *revanche* acquired the power, and soon the Germans found in their rear an army of a million bayonets. Finding itself be- tween the hammer and the anvil, the German Army was compelled to accept the honourable terms of peace offered to it by the Chinese Emperor. The exultant Frenchmen, fraternising with the yellow men, scattered over Germany and soon lost all notion of military discipline. The Emperor ordered his army to cut up allies who were no longer useful, and with Chinese punctiliousness the order was exactly carried out. Simultaneously in Paris workmen *sans patrie* organised a rising, and the capital of Western culture joyfully opened its gates to the Lord of the East. His curiosity satisfied, the Emperor set off to Boulogne, where, protected by the fleet that had come round from the Pacific, transports were speedily prepared for ferrying his army over to England. He was short of money, however, and so the English succeeded in buying him off with a sum of one milliard pounds. In a year's time all the European States submitted as vassals to the domination of the Chinese Emperor, who, having left sufficient troops in Europe, returned to the East in order to organise naval expeditions against America and Australia.

The new Mongolian yoke over Europe lasted for half a century. In the inner forms of life this epoch was marked by a general confusion and deep mutual permeation of European and Eastern ideas, provid- ing a repetition on a grand scale of the ancient Alexandrian syncretism. The most characteristic facts in the practical walks of life were three: the great influx into Europe of Chinese and Japanese workmen and the consequent acuteness of social and economic problems; the continued activity of the ruling classes in the way of palliative attempts in order to solve those problems; and, lastly, the in- creased activity of secret international societies, organising a great European conspiracy for expel- ling the Mongols and re-establishing the indepen- dence of Europe. This [colossal conspiracy, which was supported by the local national governments, in so far as they could evade the control of the

Emperor's legates, was organised in masterly fashion and was crowned with most brilliant success. An appointed hour saw the beginning of a massacre of the Mongolian soldiers, and of annihilation and expulsion of the Asiatic workmen. Secret bodies of European troops were suddenly revealed in various places, and a general mobilisation was car- ried out according to plans previously prepared. The new Emperor, who was a grandson of the great conqueror, hurried from China to Russia, but his innumerable hordes suffered a crushing defeat at the hands of the All-European Army. Their scat- tered remnants returned to the interior of Asia, and Europe breathed freely again. The long submission to the Asiatic barbarians due to the disunity of the States, which troubled themselves only about their own national interests, was now over, brought to an end by an international organisation of the whole of the European population. As a natural conse- quence of this fact, the old traditional organisation of individual States was everywhere deprived of its former importance, and the last traces of ancient monarchical institutions gradually disappeared. Europe in the twenty-first century represented an alliance of more or less democratic nations the United States of Europe. The progress of material culture, somewhat interrupted by the Mongolian yoke and the war of liberation, now burst forth with a greater force. The problems of inner consciousness, however, such as the questions of life and death, the ultimate destiny of the world and mankind, made more complicated and involved by the latest researches and discoveries in the fields of psychology and physiology—these as before remained unsolved. Only one important, though negative, result made itself apparent: it was the final bankruptcy of the materialistic theory. The notion of the universe as a system of dancing atoms, and of life as the result of mechanical accumulation of the slightest changes in materia, no longer satisfied a single reasoning intellect. Mankind had outgrown that stage of philosophical infancy. On the other side, it became equally evident that it had also outgrown the in- fantile capacity for a naive, unconscious faith. Such ideas as God, *creating* the universe *out of nothing*, were no longer taught even at elementary schools. A certain high level of ideas concerning" such sub- jects had been evolved, and no dogmatism could risk a descent below it. And though the majority of thinking people had remained faithless, the few believers had of necessity become thinking, thus fulfilling the commandment of the Apostle: "Be infants in your hearts, but not in your reason."

At that time there was among the few believing spiritualists a remarkable man—many called him a superman—who was equally far both from infantile intellect and infantile heart. He was still young, but owing to his great genius, at the age of thirty- three he already became famous as a great thinker, writer, and politician. Conscious of the great power of spirit in himself, he was always a confirmed spiritualist, and his clear intellect always showed him the truth of what one should believe in: good, God, Messiah. In this he *believed,* but he *loved* only *himself.* He believed in God, but at the bottom of his heart he involuntarily and unconsciously pre- ferred himself to Him. He believed in good, but the all-seeing eye of the Eternal knew thaCthis would bow down before Evil as soon as it bribed him—not by a deception of senses and base pas- sions, not even by the bait of power, but only by his own unutterable self-love. This self-love was neither an unconscious instinct nor an insane ambi- tion. Apart from his exceptional genius, beauty, and nobility of character, the reserve, disinterested- ness, and active sympathy with those in need, which he evinced to such a great extent, seemed abundantly to justify the immense self-love of this great spiritualist, ascetic, and philanthropist. Did he deserve blame because, being, as he was, so gener- ously supplied with the gifts of God, he saw in them the signs of Heaven's special benevolence to him, and thought himself to be second only to God himself? In a word, he considered himself to be what Christ in reality was. But this conception of his higher value showed itself in practice not in the exercise of his moral duty to God and the world, but in seizing his privilege and advantage at the expense of others, and of Christ in particular.

At first he had no ill-feeling towards Christ. He recognised His Messianic importance and value, but he was sincere in seeing in Him only his own greatest precursor the moral achievement of Christ and His uniqueness were beyond an intel- lect so completely clouded by self-love as his. He reasoned thus: "Christ came before me. I come second. But what in order of time appears later is in its essence of greater importance. I come last at the end of history for the very reason that I am most perfect. I am the final saviour of the world, and Christ—is my precursor. His mission was to precede and prepare for my coming." So thinking, the superman of the twenty-first century applied to himself everything that was said in the Gospels about the second advent, explaining the latter not as a return of the same Christ, but as a replacing of the preliminary Christ by the final one—that is, by himself.

At this stage the coming man presented few characteristic or original features. His attitude to Christ resembled, for instance, that of Mahomed, a truthful man, against whom no charge of harbouring evil designs can be brought.

Yet in another way this man justified his selfish preference of himself before Christ. "Christ," he said, "preaching and practising in life moral good, was a reformer of mankind, whereas I am called to be the *benefactor* of that same mankind, partly reformed and partly incapable of being reformed. I will give all men what they require. As a moralist.

Christ divided men by the notion of good and evil. I shall unite them by benefits which are as much needed by good as by evil people. I shall be the true representative of that God who maketh His sun to shine upon the good and the evil, and who maketh the rain fall upon the just and upon the unjust. Christ brought the sword; I shall bring peace. He threatened the earth with the Day of Judgment. But the last judge will be myself, and my judgment will be not only that of justice, but also that of mercy. The justice that will be meted out in my sentences will not be a retributive justice, however, but a distributive one. I shall judge every man according to his deserts, and shall give every-body what he needs."

In this magnificent spirit he now waited for God to call him in some unmistakable fashion to take upon himself the work of saving mankind; for some obvious and striking testimony that he was the elder son, the beloved first-born child of God. He waited and sustained himself by the consciousness of his superhuman virtues and gifts, for he, as was said, was a man of irreproachable morals and exceptional genius.

Thus this just but proud man waited for the sanc-tion of the Most High to begin his saving of man-kind; but he could see no signs of it. He had passed the age of thirty. Three more years passed by. A thought suddenly leaps into his mind and thrilled him to the core. "What," thought he, "what if by some accident it is not I, but the other one . . . the Galilean. If He is not my annunciator but the true deliverer, the first and the last one? But in that case He must be alive. . . . Where is He, then? What if He suddenly comes to me. . . here, presently? What shall I tell Him? Shall I not be compelled to kneel down before Him as the very last silly Christian, as some Russian peasant who mutters without understanding: 'Lord, Jesus Christ, forgive me, a sinful man!' And it will be I, the serene genius, the superman! It cannot be!" And here, instead of his former reasoning and cold reverence to God and Christ, a sudden fear was born and grew in his heart, next followed by a burning *envy* consuming all his being, and by an ardent hatred that takes the very breath away. "It is I, it is I, and not He! He is dead, is and will ever be! He did not—no, did not rise! His body saw cor-ruption in the grave as that of the very last. . . ." And, his mouth foaming, he rushed in convulsive movements out of the house, through the garden, and ran along a rocky path covered by the dark gloomy night.

His rage calmed down and gave place to a despair, dry and heavy as the rocks, sombre as the night. He stopped in front of a sharp precipice, from the bottom of which he could hear the faint sounds of the stream running over the stones. An unbearable anguish pressed upon his heart. Sud-denly a thought flashed across his mind. "Shall I call Him? Shall I ask Him what to do?" And in the midst of darkness he could see a pale and grief-stained image. "He pities me. . . . Oh, no, never! He did not rise! He did not! He did not!" And he leapt from the precipice. But here something firm like a column of water held him up in the air. He felt a shock as if of electricity, and some unknown force hurled him back. For a moment he became unconscious. When he came to his senses he found himself kneeling down a few paces from the brow of the precipice. A strange figure gleaming with a dim phosphorescent light loomed up before him, and its two eyes pierced his soul with their painful penetrating glitter. He saw these two piercing eyes and heard some unfamiliar voice coming from the inside or the outside of him— he could not tell which—a—dull, muffled voice, yet distinct, metallic and expressionless as from a gramophone. And the voice said to him: "Oh, my beloved son! Let all my benevolence rest on thee! Why didst not thou seek for me? Why hast thou stooped to worship that other, the bad one, and his father ? I am thy god and father. And that crucified mendicant—he is a stranger both to me and to thee. I have no other son but thee. Thou art the sole, the only one Begotten, the equal of myself. I love thee, and ask for nothing from thee. Thou art already beautiful, great, and mighty. Do thy work in *thine* own name, not mine. I harbour no envy of thee. I love thee. I require nothing of thee.

He whom thou regardest as a God, demanded from His son an absolute obedience—even to death on a cross—and even there He did not help Him. I demand from thee nothing, and I will help thee. For the sake of thyself, for the sake of thine own dignity and excellency, and for the sake of my own disinterested love of thee, I will help thee! Receive thou my spirit! As before my spirit gave birth to thee in *beauty*, so now it gives birth to thee in *power*." With these words of the stranger, the mouth of the superman involuntarily opened, two piercing eyes came close up to his face, and he felt an icy breath which pervaded the whole of his being. At the same time he felt in himself such strength, vigour, lightness, and joy as he had never before experienced. At the same moment the luminous image and the two eyes suddenly disappeared, something lifted the man up in the air, and brought him down in his own garden, before the very doors of his house.

Next day the visitors of the great man, and even his servants, were startled by his inspired air. They would have been even more startled could they have seen with what supernatural quickness and facility he was writing, locked up in his study, his famous work entitled, "The Open Way to the Universal Peace and Well-being."

The previous books and the public activity of the superman had always met with severe criticisms, though these came chiefly from men of exceptionally deep religious convictions, who for that very reason possessed no authority, and were hardly listened to when they tried to point out in everything that the "Coming Man" wrote or said the signs of quite an exceptional and excessive self-love, and a complete absence of true simplicity, frankness, and sincerity.

But now with his new book he brought over to his side even some of his former critics and adver- saries. This book, composed after the incident at the precipice, evinced a greater power of genius than he had ever shown before. It was a work that embraced everything and solved every problem. The noble respect of the ancient traditions and symbols stood in it side by side with a bold and thorough radicalism in the sphere of social and political problems, an unlimited freedom of thought with the most profound appreciation of everything mystic, the absolute individualism with an ardent fidelity to the common weal, the most lofty idealism of the guiding principles with the perfect definite- ness in practical necessities of life. And all this was blended and cemented with such artistic genius that every thinker and every man of action, however one-sided he *may* have been, could easily view and accept the whole from his particular individual standpoint without sacrificing anything to the *truth itself,* without actually rising above his Ego, without in *reality* renouncing his one-sided ness, without correcting the inadequacy of his view and wishes, without making up their deficiencies

This wonderful book was immediately translated into the languages of all the civilised nations, and many of the uncivilised ones as well. During the whole year thousands of papers in all parts of the world were filled with the publishers' advertisements and the eulogies of the critics. Cheap editions with portraits of the author were sold in millions of copies, and all the civilised world—and now it stood for nearly all the globe—resounded with the glory of the incomparable, the great, the only one! Nobody raised his voice against the book. On every side it was accepted as the revelation of the all-complete truth. In it all the past was given its full and due justice, all the present was appraised with such impartiality and catholicity, and the happiest future was brought near in such a con- vincing and practical manner that everybody could not help saying: "Here at last we have what we need. Here is the ideal, which is not an Utopia. Here is a scheme which is not a dream." And the wonderful author not only impressed all, but he was agreeable to everybody, so that the word of Christ was fulfilled: "I have come in the name of the Father, and you accept me not. *Another* will come in his own name—him you *will* accept." For it is necessary to be *agreeable* to be accepted.

It is true some pious men, whilst praising the book whole-heartedly, had been asking why the name of Christ was never mentioned in it; but other Christians had rejoined: "So much the better.

Everything sacred has already been stained enough in the past ages to make a deeply religious author extremely careful in these matters. Then the book is imbued with the true Christian spirit of active love and all-embracing goodwill. And what more do you want?" And everybody agreed.

Soon after the publication of "The Open Way," which made its author the most popular man that had ever lived on earth, an international constitu- tional congress of the United States of Europe was to be held in Berlin. This Union, founded after a series of international and civil wars which had been brought about by the liberation from the Mongolian yoke, and had resulted in considerable alteration in the map of Europe, was now menaced with peril, not through conflicts of nations, but through the internal strife between various political and social parties. The heads of general European politics, who belonged to the powerful brotherhood of Free masons, experienced certain insufficiency of execu- tive power. The European unity obtained at such a great cost was every moment threatening to fall to pieces. There was no unanimity in the

Union Council or "*Comité permanent universel*" as not all the seats were in the hands of true masons. The independent members of the Council were entering into separate agreements, and things seemed to be drifting to another war. The "initiated" then de- cided to establish a personal executive power endowed with some considerable authority. The principal candidate was the secret member of the Order—"the Coming Man." He was the only man with a great world-wide fame. Being by profession a learned artilleryman, and by his source of income a rich capitalist, he was on friendly terms with many a financier and military man. In another, less enlightened time, there might have been put against him the fact of his extremely obscure origin. His mother, a lady of doubtful reputation, was very well known in both hemispheres, but the number of people who had grounds to consider him as their son was rather too great. These circumstances, however, could not carry any weight with the age which was so advanced as to be actually the last one. "The Coming Man" was almost unanimously elected president of the United States of Europe for life. And when he appeared on the platform in all the glamour of young super-human beauty and power, and with inspired eloquence expounded his universal programme, the assembly was carried away by the spell of his personality, and in an outburst of enthusiasm decided, even without voting, to give him the highest honour, and to elect him Roman Emperor.

The congress closed amidst general rejoicing, and the great elector published a manifesto, which . began with the words: "Nations of the World! I give you my peace," and concluded, "Nations of the World! The promises have been fulfilled! An eternal universal peace has been secured. Every attempt to destroy it will meet with a determined and irresistible opposition, since a Power is now established on earth which is stronger than all the other Powers, separately or conjointly. This incon- querable, all surmountable power belongs to me, the authorised elector of Europe, the Emperor of all its forces. International law has at last secured the sanction which was so long missing. Henceforth no Power will dare to say 'War' when I say 'Peace!' Peoples of the world, peace to you!" This mani- festo had the desired effect. Everywhere outside Europe, particularly in America, powerful im- perialist parties were formed which compelled their Governments to join the United States of Europe under the supreme authority of the Roman Em- peror. There still remained a few independent tribes and little States in remote parts of Asia and Africa, but with a small but chosen army of Russian, German, Polish, Hungarian, and Turkish regiments the Emperor set out for a military march from the Eastern Asia to Morocco, and without much blood- shed brought under subjection all the insubordinate States. In all the countries of the two hemispheres he installed his viceroys, choosing them from among the native nobles who had been educated in European fashion and were faithful to him. In all the heathen countries the native population, greatly impressed and charmed by his personality, pro- claimed him as their supreme god. In a single year a real universal monarchy in the true and proper sense of the word was established. The germs of wars were radically destroyed. The Universal League of Peace met for the last time, and having delivered an exalted panegyric to the Great Peace- maker, dissolved itself as being no longer necessary. On the eve of the second year of his reign the World's Emperor published a new manifesto: "Nations of the World! I have promised you peace, and I have given it you. But peace is joyful only through prosperity. Who in peace-time is threatened with poverty has no pleasure in peace. I call, therefore, all the cold and hungry ones to come to me, and I will give them food and warmth!" Here he announced a simple and com- prehensive social reform which had already been enunciated in his book, and which then captured all the noble and sound minds. Now, owing to the concentration in his hands of the money resources of the world and of the colossal land properties, he could carry into effect that reform in accordance with the wishes of the poor and without causing much pain to the rich. Everybody now received according to his talents, and every talent according to its work and merit.

The new lord of the world before everything else was a kind-hearted philanthropist, and not only a philanthropist, but even a *philozoist*. He was a vegetarian himself, prohibited vivisection, and insti- tuted a strict supervision over slaughter-houses; whilst societies for protecting animals received from him every encouragement. But what was more important than these details, the most fundamental form of equality was firmly established among man-kind, the *equality of universal satiety*. This took place in the second year of his reign. Social and economic problems had been finally settled. But if satisfaction is a question of primary importance for the hungry, the satisfied ones crave for something else. Even satiated animals usually want not only to sleep, but also to play. The more so with man-kind which has always *post panem* craved for *circenses*.

The Emperor-superman understood what his mob wanted. At that time a great magician, en-wrapped in a dense cloud of strange facts and wild stories, came to him in Rome from the Far East. The rumour spread amongst the neo-Buddhists credited him with a divine origin from the god of Sun Suria and some river nymph.

This magician, Apollonius by name, was doubt-less a man of genius. A semi-Asiatic and a semi-European, a catholic bishop in *partibus infidelium*, he combined in himself in a most striking manner the knowledge of the latest conclusions and appli-cations of Western science with the art of utilising all that was really sound and important in the tradi-tional mysticism of the East. The results of this combination were startling. Apollonius learned amongst other things the semi-scientific and semi-mystic art of attracting and directing at will the atmospheric electricity, and the people said of him that he could *bring down fire from heaven*. However, though startling the imagination of the crowd by various unheard of phenomena, for some time he did not abuse his power for any special selfish ends.

It was this man who came to the great Emperor, saluted him as the true son of God, declared that he had discovered in the secret books of the East cer-tain unmistakable prophecies pointing to the Em-peror as the last saviour and judge of the Universe, and offered him his services and all his art. The Emperor, completely charmed by the man, accepted him as a gift from above, decorated him with all kinds of gorgeous titles and made him his constant companion. So the nations of the world, after they had received from their lord universal peace and universal abolition of hunger, were now given the possibility of never-ending enjoyment of most diverse and extraordinary miracles. Thus came to end the third year of the reign of the superman.

After the happy solution of political and social problems, the religious question was brought to the front. This was raised by the Emperor himself, and in the first place in its application to Christianity. At the time the position of Christianity was as follows : Its followers had greatly diminished in numbers and barely included forty-five million men in the whole world; but morally it made a marked progress, and gained in quality what it lost in numbers. Men who were not bound up with Christianity by any spiritual tie were no longer recorded amongst the Christians. Various Christian persua- sions fairly equally diminished in their numbers, so that the proportional relationship amongst them was maintained almost unchanged. As to mutual feel- ings, hostility did not entirely give place to amity, but considerably softened down, and points of dis- agreement lost much of their former acuteness. The Papacy had been long before expelled from Rome, and after long wanderings had found refuge in St. Petersburg on condition that it refrained from propaganda there, and in the country. In Russia it soon became greatly simplified. Leaving prac- tically unchanged the number of its colleges and offices, it was obliged to infuse into their work a more fervent spirit, and to cut down to the smallest limits its pompous ritual and ceremonial. Many strange and seductive customs, though not formally abolished, fell of themselves into disuse. In all the other countries, particularly in North America, the Catholic priesthood still had a good many repre- sentatives, possessed of strong will, inexhaustible energy and independent character, who welded to- gether the Catholic Church into a closer unity than it had ever been before, and who preserved for it its international, cosmopolitan importance. As to Pro- testantism, which was still led by Germany, especially since the union of the greater part of the Anglican church with the Catholic one—this had freed itself from its extreme negative tendencies, the followers of which openly went over to the camp of religious apathy and unbelief. The Evangelical church now contained only the sincerely religious, headed by men who combined a vast learning with a deep religious feeling, and an ever-growing desire to bring to life again in their own persons the living spirit of the true ancient Christianity. Rus- sian orthodoxy, after political events had altered the official position of the Church, lost many millions, of its sham nominal members; but it won the joy of unification with the best part of the "old believers," and even many of the positively religious sectarians. This renovated Church, though not increasing in numbers, began to grow in strength of spirit, which it particularly revealed in its struggle with the numerous sects, not entirely devoid of the de- moniacal and satanic element, which found root among the people and in society.

During the first two years of the new reign, all Christians, frightened at, and weary of, the number of preceding revolutions and wars, looked upon their new lord and his peaceful reforms partly with a benevolent expectation, and partly with an unre- served, sympathetic, and even a fervent enthusiasm. But in the third year, after the great magician had made his appearance, serious fears and antipathy began to grow in the minds of many an orthodox Catholic and Protestant. The Gospel and Apostolic texts speaking of the Prince of this Age and of Anti-Christ were now read more carefully and led to lively comments. The Emperor soon perceived from certain signs that a storm was brewing, and resolved to bring the matter to a head without any further delay. In the beginning of the fourth year of his reign he published a manifesto to all his true Christians, without distinction of churches, inviting them to elect or appoint authoritative representatives for the World's Congress to be held under his presidency. At that time the imperial residence was transferred from Rome to Jerusalem. Palestine was already an autonomous province, inhabited and governed mainly by the Jews. Jerusalem was a free and now an imperial city. The Christian shrines remained unmolested, but over the whole of the large platform of Haram-esh-Sheriff, extending from Birket-Israin and the barracks right to the mosque of El-Ax and the " Solomon's Stables," there was erected an immense building, which incor- porated in itself, besides the two small ancient mosques, a huge " Empire " temple for the unifica- tion of all cults, and two luxurious imperial palaces, with libraries, museums, and special apartments for magic experiments and exercises. It was in this half-temple, half-palace that the World's Congress was to meet on September 14th. As the evangelical church has no hierarchy in the proper sense of the word, the Catholic and orthodox hierarchs, in com- pliance with the express wish of the Emperor, and in order that a greater uniformity of representation should obtain, decided to admit to the proceedings of the congress a certain number of lay members. Once, however, these were admitted, it seemed impos- sible to exclude from the congress the clergy, both of the monastic and secular order. In this way the total number of members at the congress exceeded three thousand, whilst about half a million Christian pilgrims flooded Jerusalem and all Palestine. Amongst the members present three men were par- ticularly conspicuous. The first was Pope Peter II., who in true right led the Catholic part of the con- gress. His predecessor died on the way to the congress, and a conclave met in Damascus, which unanimously elected Cardinal Simone Barionini, who took the name of Peter. He came of plebeian stock, from the province of Naples, and became famous as a preacher of the Carmelite Order, having earned great successes in fighting a certain Satanic sect which was spreading in St. Petersburg and its environs, and seducing not only the orthodox, but the Catholic men as well. Raised to the archbishopric of Magilov and next to the Cardinal's chair, he was all along marked for the tiara. He was a man of fifty, of middle stature and strongly built, had a red face, a crooked nose, and thick eyebrows. He had an impulsive and ardent temperament, spoke with fervour and with sweeping gesticulations, and enthused more than convinced his audience. The new Pope had no trust in the Emperor, and looked at him with a disapproving eye, particularly since the deceased Pope, yielding to the Emperor's pressure, made a cardinal of the Imperial Chancellor and great magician of the world, the exotic Bishop Apollonius, whom Peter regarded as a doubtful Catholic and a doubtless fraud. The actual, though not official, leader of the orthodox members was Eldeir John, extremely well known amongst the Russian people. Officially he was considered a bishop "in retirement," but he did not live in any monastery, being always engaged in travelling all over the world. Many legendary stories were circulated about him. Some people believed that he was Feodor Kusmich, that is, Emperor Alexander I., who had died three centuries back and was now raised to life. Others went further and maintained that he was the true Elder John, that is, John the Apostle, who had never died and openly reappeared in the later times. He him- self said nothing about his origin and younger days. Now he was a very old but vigorous man, with white hair and beard tinged with a yellowish and even greenish colour, tall in stature, and thin in the body, but with full and slightly rosy cheeks, vivid sparkling eyes and a tender and kind expression in his face and speech. He was always dressed in a white cassock and mantle. At the head of the evangelical members of the congress was the most learned Ger- man theologian, Professor Ernst Pauli. He was a short, wizened, little old man, with a huge forehead, sharp nose, and cleanly-shaven chin. His eyes were distinguished by their peculiarly ferocious and yet at one and the same time kindly gaze. He inces- santly rubbed his hands, shook his head, sternly knitted his brows and pursed up his lips; whilst with eyes all flashing he sternly ejaculated: "So! Nun! Ja! So also!" His dress bore all the appearance of solemnity—a white tie and long pas- toral frock-coat decorated with signs of his order.

The opening of the congress was very imposing. Two-thirds of the immense temple, devoted to the "unification of all the cults," were covered with benches and other sitting accommodation for mem- bers of the congress. The remaining third was taken by the high platform, on which were placed the Emperor's throne, another a little below it intended for the great magician—also the cardinal- imperial chancellor; and behind them rows of arm- chairs for the ministers, courtiers, and State officials, whilst along the side there were the still longer rows of armchairs, the intended occupants of which remained undisclosed. The gallery was taken by the orchestra, whilst in the adjoining square there were installed two regiments of the Guards and a battery for triumphal salutes. The members of the congress had already attended their services in their various churches, and the opening of the congress was to be entirely civil. When the Emperor, accom- panied by the great magician and his suite, made his entrance, the band began to play the " March of Unified Mankind," which was the international hymn of the Empire, and all the members rose to their feet, and waving their hats, gave three enthusi- astic cheers: "Vivat! Hurrah! Hoch!" The Emperor, standing by the throne and stretching for- ward his hand with the air of majestic benevolence, said in a sonorous and pleasing voice: "Christians of all sects! My beloved subjects and brothers! From the beginning of my reign, which the Most High blessed with such wonderful and glorious deeds, I have never had any cause to be dissatisfied with you. You have always performed your duties true to your faith and conscience. But this is no.t sufficient for me. My sincere love to you, my be- loved brothers, thirsts for reciprocation. I wish you to recognise me your true leader in every enterprise undertaken for the well-being of mankind, not merely out of your sense of duty to me, but mainly out of your heartfelt love for me. So now, besides what I generally do for all, I am about to show you my special benevolence. Christians! What can I bestow upon you? What can I give you, not as my subjects, but as my co-religionists, my brothers! Christians! Tell me what is the most precious thing for you in Christianity, so that I may direct my efforts to that end?" He stopped for a time, wait- ing for an answer. The hall was filled with rever- berating muffled sounds. The members of the con- gress were consulting each other. Pope Peter, with fervent gesticulations, was explaining something to his followers. Professor Pauli was shaking his head and ferociously smacking with his lips. Elder John bending over an Eastern bishop and a Capucin quietly tried to impress something upon them. After he had waited a few minutes, the Emperor again addressed the congress in the same kind tone, in which, however, there could be sounded a scarcely perceptible note of irony: "My kind Christians," said he, "I understand how difficult it is for you to give me a direct answer. I will help you also in this. From time immemorial, unfortunately, you have been broken up into various confessions and sects, so that you perhaps have scarcely one com- mon object of desire. But if you cannot agree amongst yourselves, I hope I shall be able to show agreement with you all by bestowing upon all your sections the same love and the same readiness to satisfy the *true* desire of each one of them. Kind Christians! I know that to many, and not the last ones amongst you, the most precious thing in Christianity is the *spiritual authority* with which it endows its legal representatives—of course, not for their personal benefit, but for the common weal, since on this authority the right spiritual order and moral discipline so necessary for everybody, firmly rest. Kind brothers-Catholic! How well do I understand your view, and how much would I like to base my imperial power on the authority of your spiritual chief ! Lest you should think that this is a mere flattery and windy words we most solemnly declare: by virtue of our autocratic power the Supreme Bishop of all the Catholics, the Pope of Rome, is henceforth restored to his throne in Rome, with all the former rights and privileges belonging to this title and chair, given at any time by our pre- decessors, from Constantine the Great onwards. For this, brothers-Catholic, I wish to receive from you only your inner heart-felt recognition of my- self as your sole protector and patron. Whoever of those present here does recognise me as such in his heart and conscience, let him come up here to this side!" Here he pointed to the empty seats on the platform. And instantly, nearly all the princes of the Catholic Church, cardinals and bishops, the greater part of the laymen and over a half of the monks, shouting in exultation: "Gratias agimus! Domine! Salvum fac magnum imperatorem!" rose to the platform and, humbly bowing their heads to the Emperor, took their seats. Below, however, in the middle of the hall, straight and immovable, like a marble statue, sat in his seat Pope Peter II. All those who had surrounded him were now on the platform. But the diminished crowd of monks and laymen who remained below moved nearer and closed in a dense crowd around him. And one could hear the subdued mutter issuing from them: "Non praevalebunt, non praevalebunt portae inferni."

With a startled look cast at the immovable Pope, the Emperor again raised his voice: "Kind brothers! I know that there are amongst you many for whom the most precious thing in Christianity is its *sacred tradition*—the old symbols, the old hymns and prayers, the ikons and the old ritual.

Indeed, what can be more precious for a religious soul? Know, then, my beloved ones, that to-day I have signed the decree and have set aside vast sums of money for the establishment in our glorious Empire city, Constantinople, of a world's museum of Christian archaeology, with the object of collecting, studying, and saving all the monuments of church antiquity, more particularly of the Eastern one; and I ask you to select from your midst a committee for working out with me the measures which are to be carried out, so that the modern life, morals, and customs may be organised as nearly as possible in accordance with the traditions and institutions of the Holy Orthodox Church. My orthodox brothers! Those of you who view with favour this will of mine, who can in their inner consciousness call me their true leader and lord—let those come up here." Here the greater part of the hierarchs of the East and North, and more than a half of the orthodox clergymen, monks, and laymen, rose with joyful exclamation to the platform, casting suspicious eyes at the Catholics, who were already proudly occupy- ing their seats. But Elder John remained in his place, and sighed loudly. And when the crowd round him became greatly thinned, he left his bench and went over to Pope Peter and his group. He was followed by the other orthodox members who did not go to the platform. Then the Emperor spoke again: "I am aware, kind Christians, that there are amongst you also such who place the greatest value upon the personal confidence in truth and the free examination of the Scriptures. How I view this, there is no need for me to enlarge upon at the moment. You are perhaps aware that even in my youth I wrote a big book on the Higher Criticism, which at that time excited much comment and laid the foundation of my popularity. In memory of this, I presume, the University of Tubingen only the other day requested me to accept the degree of a Doctor of Theology *honoris causa*. I have replied that I accept it with pleasure and gratitude. And to-day, simultaneously with the decree of the Museum of Christian Archaeology, I signed another decree establishing a world's institute for free examination of the Scriptures from all sides and in all directions, and for study of all subsidiary sciences, to which an annual sum of one and a half million marks is granted. I call those of you who look with sincere favour at this my act of goodwill, and are able in their true feeling to recognise me their sovereign leader, to come up here to the new Doctor of Theology." A strange but hardly per- ceptible smile changed the beautiful mouth of the great man when he concluded this speech. More than half of the learned theologians were moving to the platforms, though somewhat slowly and hesitatingly. Everybody looked at Professor Pauli, who seemed to be rooted to his seat. He dropped his head, bent down and shrank. The learned theologians who had already managed to get on the platform seemed to feel very awkward, and one of them even suddenly dropped his hand in renuncia- tion, and, having jumped right down past the stairs, ran hobbling to Professor Pauli and the members who remained with him. At this the Professor raised his head, got up on his feet as if without a definite object in view, and then walked past the empty benches, accompanied by his co-religionists who withstood the temptation, and took his seat near Elder John and Pope Peter with their followers. The greater part of the members, including nearly all the hierarchs of the East and West, were now on the platform. Below there remained only the three groups of members now more closely brought together, who clung around to Elder John, Pope Peter, and Professor Pauli.

In a grieved voice the Emperor addressed them: "What else can I do for you, you strange people? What do you want from me? I cannot understand. Tell me yourselves, you Christians, deserted by the majority of your brothers and leaders, condemned by popular sentiment: what is it that you value most in Christianity?" At this Elder John rose up like a white candle, and said in a quiet voice: "Great sovereign! The thing we value most in Christianity is Christ Himself—He in His person. All the rest cometh from Him, for we know that in Him dwelleth bodily the whole fulness of Divinity. But we are ready, sire, to accept any gift from you as well, if only we recognise the holy hand of Christ in your generosity. Our candid answer to your question, what you can do for us, is this: Here, now and before us, name the name of Jesus Christ, the Son of God, who came in the flesh, rose, and is coming again—name His name, and we will accept you with love as the true forerunner of

His second glorious coming." He finished his speech and fixed his eyes on the face of the Emperor. A terrible change had come over it. A hellish storm was raging within him, like the one he experienced on that fateful night. He had entirely lost his mental balance, and was concentrating all his thoughts on preserving control over his appearance, so that he should not betray himself before the time. He was making superhuman efforts not to throw himself, yelling wildly, on Elder John and begin tearing him with his teeth. Suddenly he heard a familiar, un- earthly voice: "Keep silent and fear nothing! He remained silent. Only his face, livid like death, looked distorted and his eyes flashed. In the meantime, while Elder John was still making his speech, the great magician, wrapped in his ample tri-coloured mantle, which concealed nearly the whole of his car- dinal purple, could be noticed to be busy doing some- thing underneath it. His eyes were fixed and flash- ing, and his lips slightly moving. It could be seen through the open windows of the temple that an immense black cloud was covering the sky, and soon a complete darkness set in. Elder John, startled and frightened, stared at the face of the silent Emperor, when he suddenly sprang back, and turning to his followers shouted in a stifled voice: "My dearest ones, it is Anti-Christ!" At this moment, followed by a deafening thunderclap, a great thunderbolt flashed into the temple and struck Elder John. Everyone was stupefied for a second, and when the deafened Christians came to their senses, Elder John was seen lying dead on the floor.

The Emperor, pale but calm, spoke to the assembly: "You have witnessed the judgment of God. I had no wish to take any man's life, but thus my Heavenly Father avenges His beloved son. It is finished. Who will oppose the will of the Most High ? Secretaries, write down: The Œcumenical Council of All Christians, after an insensate oppo- nent of the Divine Majesty had been struck by fire from heaven, recognised unanimously the sovereign Emperor of Rome and all the Universe its supreme leader and lord." Suddenly a word, loudly distinct, passed throughout the temple: "Contradicatur!" Pope Peter II. rose, and with face empurpled and his body trembling with indignation, lifted up his stick in the direction of the Emperor. "Our only Lord," shouted he,

" is Jesus Christ, the Son of the living God! And who thou art, thou heardest just now. Away thou Cain, thou murderer! Get thee gone, thou incarnation of the Devil! By the authority of Christ, I, the servant of God's servants, for ever expel thee, thou foul dog, from the precincts of God, and cast thee out to thy father Satan! Anathema! Anathema! Anathema! "While he was so speaking, the great magician was moving restlessly under his mantle, and louder than the last" Anathema!" the thunder rumbled, and the last Pope fell lifeless on the floor. "So die all my enemies by the arm of my Father!" said the Emperor. "Pereant, pereant!" exclaimed the trembling princes of the Church. The Emperor turned round, and, supported by the great magician and accompanied by all his crowd, slowly walked out to the door at the back of the platform. There remained in the temple only the corpses and a little knot of Christians half-dead from fear. The only person who did not lose control over himself was Professor Pauli. The general horror seemed to have raised in him all the powers of his spirit. He even changed in appearance; his countenance became noble and inspired. With determined steps he walked up on to the platform, took one of the seats previously occupied by some State official, and began to write on a sheet of paper. When he had finished he got up and read out in a loud voice: "In the glory of our only saviour, Jesus Christ! The Œcumenical Council of our Lord's churches, which met at Jerusalem after our most blessed brother John, the representative of Christianity of the East, had exposed the arch-deceiver and the enemy of God as the true Anti-Christ, foretold in the word of God, and after our most blessed father Peter, the representative of Christianity of the West, had lawfully and justly expelled him for ever from the Church of God, now in the face of the corpses of these two witnesses of Christ, murdered for the truth, resolves: To cease any communion with the excommunicated one and with his foul crowd, and to go to the desert and to wait for the inevitable coming of our true Lord, Jesus Christ." The crowd was seized with enthusiasm, and loud exclamations could be heard on all sides. "Adveniat! Adveniat cito! Komm, Herr Jesu, komm! Come, Lord Jesus Christ!"

Professor Pauli wrote again and read: "Accept- ing unanimously this first and last deed of the last Œcumenical Council, we sign our names"—and here he invited those present to do so. All hurried to the platform and signed their names. And last in the list stood in big Gothic characters the signature: "Duorum defunctorum testium locum tenens Ernst Pauli." "Now let us go with our ark of the last covenant," said he, pointing to the two deceased. The corpses were put on stretchers. Slowly, sing-ing Latin, German and Church-Slavonic hymns, the Christians walked to the gate leading out from Haram-esh-Sheriff. Here the procession was stopped by one of the Emperor's officials, who was accompanied by a squad of the Guards. The sol- diers remained at the entrance whilst the official read: "By order of his Divine Majesty. For the enlightenment of the Christian people and for its safety from wicked men spreading unrest and temptations, we deem necessary to resolve that the corpses of the two agitators, killed by the heavenly fire, be publicly exhibited in the street of the Chris- tians (Haret-en-Nasara), at the entrance into the principal temple of this religion, called the Temple of our Lord's Sepulchre, also that of the Resurrec- tion, so that everybody may convince himself that they are really dead. Their obstinate followers, who wrathfully reject all our benefits and insanely shut their eyes to the patent signs of Deity itself—are by our mercy and presentations before our Heavenly Father, relieved from a much-deserved death by the heavenly fire, and are left at their free will with the sole prohibition, necessary for the common good, of living in towns "and other places of residence, lest they disturb and tempt innocent, simple-minded folk with their malicious fancies." When he had finished reading, eight soldiers, at the sign of the officer, came up with stretchers to the bodies.

"Let the written word be fulfilled," said Professor Pauli. And the Christians who were holding the stretchers silently passed them to the soldiers, who went away with them through the north-western gate, whilst the Christians, having gone out through the north-eastern gate, hurriedly walked from the city past the Mount of Olives to Jericho, along the road which had previously been cleared of other people by the gendarmes and two cavalry regiments. It was decided to wait a few days on the desert hills near Jericho. Next morning, friendly Christian pilgrims came from Jerusalem and told what had been going on in Sion. After the dinner at the Court all the members of the congress were invited to a vast throne hall (near the supposed site of Solo- mon's throne), and the Emperar, addressing the representatives of the Catholic hierarchy, told them that the well-being of their Church clearly demanded from them the immediate election of a worthy successor to the apostate Peter, that in the circumstances of the time the election must needs be a summary one, that his the Emperor's presence as that of the leader and representative of the whole Christian world, would amply make up for the in- evitable omissions in the ritual, and that he on behalf of all the Christians suggested that the Holy College elect his beloved friend and brother Apollonius, so that their close friendship could firmly and in- dissolubly unite Church and State for their mutual benefit. The Holy College retired to a separate room for a conclave, and in an hour and a half it returned with its new Pope Apollonius. In the meantime, while the election was being carried out, the Emperor was meekly, sagaciously, and elo- quently persuading the Orthodox and Evangelical representatives, in view of the new great era in Christian history, to put an end to their old dissen- sions, giving his word that Apollonius would be able to abolish all the abuses of the Papal authority known to history. Persuaded by this speech, the Orthodox and Protestant representatives drafted a deed of the unification of all the churches, and when Apollonius with the cardinals appeared in the hall, met by shouts of joy from all those present, a Greek bishop and an evangelical pastor presented to him their document. "Accipio et approbo et laetificatur cor meum," said Apollonius, signing it. "I am as much a true Orthodox and a Protestant as I am a true Catholic," added he, and exchanged friendly kisses with the Greek and the German. Then he came up to the Emperor, who embraced him and long held him in his arms. At this time tongues of flame began to dart about in the palace and the temple. They grew and became transformed into luminous shapes of strange beings, and flowers never seen before came down from above, filling the air with unknown aroma. Enchanting sounds of music, stirring the very depths of the soul, produced by unfamiliar instruments, were heard, while angelic voices of unseen singers sang the glory of the new lords of heaven and earth. Suddenly a terrific subterranean noise was heard in the north-western corner of the palace under "Kubbet-el-Aruah," that is "the dome of souls," where, according to the Moslem belief, the entrance to the hell was hidden. When the assembly invited by the Emperor went to that end all could clearly hear innumerable voices, thin and penetrating—either childish or devilish—which were exclaiming: "The time has come, do let us out, dear saviours, dear saviours!" But when Apollonius, kneeling on the ground, shouted some- thing down in an unknown language three times, the voices died down and the subterranean noise subsided. Meanwhile a vast crowd of people sur- rounded Haram-esh-Sheriff on all sides. Dark- ness set in and the Emperor, with the new Pope, came out upon the eastern terrace—the signal for a storm of rejoicings. The Emperor bowed affably to the people around, whilst Apollonius, taking from the huge baskets brought up by the cardinal-deacons, incessantly threw into the air, making them burn by mere touch of his hand, magnificent fireworks, rockets, and fountains, that now glimmered like phosphorescent pearls, and now sparkled with all the tints of a rainbow. On reaching the ground all the sparkles transformed into numberless variously coloured sheets containing complete and absolute indulgences of all sins—past, present, and future.[18] The popular exultation overflowed all limits. True, there were some who stated that they had seen with their own eyes the indulgences turn into hideous frogs and snakes. But the vast majority of the people were pleased immensely, and the popular festivities continued a few days longer. The prodigies of the new Pope now surpassed all imagination, so that it would be a hopeless task even to attempt a description of them. In the meantime among the desert hills of Jericho the Christians were devoting themselves to fasting and prayers.

On the night of the fourth day Professor Pauli, with nine comrades riding on asses and having a cart with them, succeeded in getting inside Jerusalem and passing through side-streets by Haram-esh-Sheriff to

---

[18] With reference to the above, see Preface. —Author.

Haret-en-Nasara, came to the entrance to the Temple of Resurrection, in front of which, on the pavement, the bodies of Pope Peter and Elder John were lying. The street was deserted at that time of night, as all the people had gone to Hasam-esh-Sheriff. The sentries were fast asleep. The party that came for the bodies found them quite untouched by decom- position, not even stiff or heavy. They put them on the stretchers covered with the cloaks they had brought with them, and by the same circuitous road went back to their followers. They had hardly lowered the stretchers to the ground when suddenly the spirit of life could be seen re-entering the deceased bodies. They moved slightly as if they were trying to throw off the cloaks in which they were wrapped. With shouts of joy everyone lent them aid, and soon both the revived men rose to their feet safe and sound. Then said Elder John: "Ah, my dear ones, we have not parted after all! I will tell you this: it is time that we carry out the last prayer of Christ about His disciples—that they should be all one, even as He Himself is one with the Father. For this unity in Christ let us honour our beloved brother Peter. Let him at last pasture the flocks of Christ. There it is, brother!" And he put his arms round Peter. Here Professor Pauli came nearer. "*Tu es Petrus!*" said he to the Pope, "*jetzt ist es ja grundlich erwiesen und ausser jedem Zweifel gesetzt.*" And he shook Peter's hand firmly with his own right hand, whilst his left hand he stretched out to John, saying: "*So also Vaterchennun sind wir ja Eins in Christo.*" In this manner the unification of churches took place in the midst of a dark night, on a high and deserted spot. But the night darkness was suddenly illuminated with brilliant light and a great sign appeared in the heavens; it was—a woman, clothed in the sun with the moon beneath her feet, and a wreath of twelve stars on her head. The apparition remained immovable for some time, and then began slowly to move in a southerly direction. Pope Peter raised his stick and exclaimed: "Here is our sign! Let us follow it!" And he walked after the apparition, accompanied by both old men and the whole crowd of the Christians, to God's mountain, to Sinai. . . .

(*Here the reader stopped.*)

LADY. Well, why don't you go on?

MR. Z. The manuscript stops here. Father Pansophius could not finish his story. He told me when he was already ill that he thought of com- pleting it "as soon as I get better," he said. But he did not get better, and the end of his story is buried with him in the graveyard of the Daniel Monastery.

LADY. But you remember what he told you, don't you? Please tell us.

MR. Z. I remember it only in the main outlines. After the spiritual leaders and representatives of Christianity had departed to the Arabian desert, whither crowds of faithful zealots of truth were streaming from all countries, the new Pope was able to corrupt unimpededly with his miracles and pro- digies all the remaining superficial Christians who were not yet disappointed with the Anti-Christ. He declared that by the power of his keys he could open the gates to other worlds. Communion of the living with the dead, and also of men with demons, became a matter of everyday occurrence, and new unheard-of forms of mystic lust and demonology began to spread amongst the people. However, the Emperor scarcely began to feel himself firmly established on religious grounds, and, yielding to the persistent suggestions of the seductive voice of the "father," had hardly declared himself the sole true incarnation of the supreme Deity of the Uni- verse, when a new trouble came upon him from a side from which nobody expected it: the Jews rose against him. This nation, which at that time reached thirty millions, was not altogether unfamiliar with the paving of the. way for the world's successes of the superman. When this latter transferred his residence to Jerusalem, secretly spreading amongst the Jews the rumour that his main object was to bring about a domination of Israel over the whole of the world, the Jews proclaimed him as their Messiah, and their exultation and devotion to him knew no bounds. And now they suddenly rose, full of wrath and thirsting for vengeance. This turn of events, doubtless foretold both in the Gospel and in the church tradition, was pictured by Father Pansophius, perhaps, with too great a simplicity and realism. You see, the Jews, who regarded the Emperor a true and perfect Israelite by blood, un- expectedly discovered that he was not even circum- cised. The same day all Jerusalem, and next day all Palestine, were up in arms against him. The boundless and fervent devotion to the saviour of Israel, the promised Messiah, gave place to as boundless and as fervent a hatred of the wily deceiver, the impudent impostor. The whole of the Jewish nation rose as one man, and its enemies were surprised to see that the soul of Israel at bottom lived not by calculations and aspirations of Mammon but by the power of an all-absorbing sentiment—the hope and strength of its eternal faith in the Messiah. The Emperor, taken by surprise at the sudden out- burst, lost all self-control, and issued a decree sentencing to death all the insubordinate Jews and Christians. Many thousands and tens of thousands who could not arm themselves in time were ruth- lessly massacred. But an army of Jews, a million strong, soon took Jerusalem, and locked up Anti- Christ in Haram-esh-Sheriff. His only support was a portion of the Guards, who were not strong enough to overwhelm the masses of the enemy. Assisted by the magic art of his Pope, the Emperor succeeded in finding his way through the besieging army, and soon appeared again in Syria at the head of an innumerable army of pagans. The Jews advanced to meet him, with little chance of gaining success. But no sooner had the outposts of the armies come in contact with each other than a terrific earthquake broke out, the crater of a tremendous volcano rose from the bottom of the Dead Sea, on the shores of which the Emperor's army had built their camp, and fiery streams mingling in a single lake of fire swal- lowed up the Emperor, all his innumerable troops, and his constant companion, Pope Apollonius, to whom even his magic art proved of no help. At the same time the Jews were running to Jerusalem in fear and horror, praying to the God of Israel to deliver them from peril. When the Holy City was already in sight, a great lightning cut the sky open from east to west, and they saw Christ descending to them clad in kingly apparel, and with the wounds from the nails on His outstretched hands. At the same time a crowd of Christians, led by Peter, John, and Paul, were moving from Sinai to Sion, and other crowds, all seized with enthusiasm, came flocking from all sides. These were all the Jews and Chris- tians executed by the Anti-Christ. They rose to life, and reigned with Christ for a thousand years.

At this point Father Pansophius thought to finish his story, which was to picture not the final cata- strophe of the Universe, but only the conclusion of our historical process. This end is the coming, the glorification, and the destruction of Anti-Christ.

POLITICIAN. And do you think that the catastrophe is very near?

MR. Z. Well, there will still be a good deal of rattling and bustling on the stage, but the drama has been all written long ago, and neither the audience nor the actors are allowed to alter anything in it.

LADY. What is, however, the ultimate meaning of this drama? I cannot understand, moreover, why your Anti-Christ hates God so much whilst in essence he is really kind and not wicked at all.

MR. Z. No. Not "in essence" That is just the point. That is the whole matter. I will withdraw the words I said before that "you cannot explain Anti-Christ only by proverbs." In point of fact, he is completely explained by a single and extremely simple proverb: "All is not gold that glitters." Of sham glitter he indeed has more than enough; but of the essential force—nothing.

GENERAL. I beg to call your attention to yet another thing. Note at what moment the curtain drops over this historical drama: it is war, a con- flict between two armies. So the end of our discus- sion comes again back to its beginning. How do you like it, Prince? Good heavens, but where is the Prince?

POLITICIAN. Didn't you observe? He quietly left us at that pathetic scene when Elder John drove the Anti-Christ into a corner. I did not want to interrupt the reading at that time, and afterwards I forgot.

GENERAL. I bet he ran away: ran away for the second time! And didn't he try to master himself? But this was too much for the poor fellow: he could not stand it for anything. Oh, dear me! dear me!

THE END

Printed for the UNIVERSITY OF LONDON PRESS. LTD., by RICHARD CLAY AND SONS, Ltd.

London and Bungay .

www.ingramcontent.com/pod-product-compliance
Lightning Source LLC
LaVergne TN
LVHW051559070426
835507LV00021B/2667